JB JOSSEY-BASS™
A Wiley Brand

Useful Policies, Forms and Examples for the Volunteer Manager

Scott C. Stevenson, Editor

WILEY

978-1-118-69194-6   ISBN

978-1-118-70404-2   ISBN (online)

Useful Policies, Examples and Forms
For the Volunteer Manager

Published by

Stevenson, Inc.

P.O. Box 4528 • Sioux City, Iowa • 51104
Phone 712.239.3010 • Fax 712.239.2166

www.stevensoninc.com

TABLE OF CONTENTS

Useful Policies, Examples and Forms for the Volunteer Manager

PROCEDURES FOR RECRUITING QUALITY VOLUNTEERS

Effective recruitment is the lifeblood of successful volunteer programs. No matter how strong or successful a program may be, attrition and turnover are challenges that must be addressed. The following articles will show you how to locate, identify and reach out to the kinds of individuals your program wants and needs as volunteers

Look for Innovative Ways to Recruit Volunteers

Looking for volunteers can be simple using the right techniques. Try these innovative volunteer recruitment techniques to bolster your volunteer base:

- **Work volunteer opportunities into public presentations.** When presenting a speech about your organization or appearing on a panel, use the opportunity to mention your agency's need for volunteers. Members of the audience are there to hear you speak and therefore interested in your organization. Ask the members of the audience to complete a sign-up sheet if they are interested in volunteering.

- **Tap volunteer organizations for volunteers.** Look to service-minded membership organizations within your community for volunteers who will assist your organization as a group. Your local Junior League, Boy or Girl Scout troops, Lions Clubs or business organizations, for example, are likely to volunteer in groups for upcoming events. Seek them out.

- **Seek to bring in young people.** Get in touch with high schools and the heads of college departments to solicit youthful volunteers for your cause.

- **Turn to employers.** Talk to personnel directors of companies, explaining in detail the volunteer opportunities available at your nonprofit. Ask if they will assist you by referring retirees and employees to volunteer at your nonprofit.

Make It Easy for Your Volunteers to Enlist Other Volunteers

Do you have a project coming up that will require two to three times the number of volunteers you presently have on hand? If so, here's a way to double or triple the number of willing participants for that special undertaking.

With a little up-front help on your part, your existing volunteers can appeal to friends, associates and family members to boost numbers for your upcoming project.

Supply each volunteer with a packet of five note cards with a preprinted message (see example at right) and coordinating envelopes. Ask them to add a handwritten salutation at the beginning of the message, sign the notes (adding a P.S. if they wish) and address the envelopes to five individuals they think would make good volunteer prospects for this onetime project. Then have them enclose the note cards, seal the envelopes, stamp them and drop them in the mail. Simple as that!

After two or three days have gone by — enough time for the recipients to have gotten their invitations — instruct the volunteers to phone their five contacts as an enlistment follow-up. Have the volunteers phone your office (or complete a return postcard that went out with the original mailing to them) to report on who agreed to help. Be sure to get new volunteers' addresses, phone numbers and e-mail addresses so your office can take it from there.

Even if you only get a 20 percent response rate, that's one new volunteer from every group of five note cards sent out. And, if every existing volunteer sent out a packet of five, you will have doubled the number of existing volunteers.

[Salutation and Name,]

I could sure use three hours of your help for a one-time project I'm working on.

As you know, I'm a regular volunteer for the West High School Boosters. On Saturday, March 22, we're hosting about 50 area high school band members (and many of their parents), who will be participating in a music contest here. It's a great opportunity for our booster association to raise needed funds for special improvements to West High.

Even though it's an all-day event, I'd really appreciate it if you could give just three hours of your time to help us out. You can either choose how you want to help or have a job assigned to you.

I'll be phoning you in the next few days to check your availability for this project.

Thank you so much for giving my request your positive consideration!

[Name and P.S.]

Tap New Volunteers by Following Who's Retiring

Do you keep track of who's approaching retirement at various businesses and organizations around your city? This can prove to be a great source of volunteers who find themselves finally having the time they want to help with worthy causes.

Maintain a tickler report of key businesses, schools and other organizations to contact at least yearly to determine who is scheduled or planning to retire in the near future. After determining who's up for retirement, send a letter of congratulations at the time of retirement and share some opportunities for volunteer involvement with your organization. Indicate that you will be phoning the retiree within the next several days to follow up.

— Who's Approaching Retirement? —
Organizations to Contact Yearly

Business or Organization	Contact Person	Phone	Person(s) Scheduled to Retire	Retirement Date	Congratulatory Letter Sent	Follow-up Call Date	Comments

Develop Plan to Attract Single Members

Single Volunteers of Northeast Ohio (Cleveland, OH) offers a simple approach to volunteerism for singles in the region by offering free membership. The organization is a social membership offering the ability for area singles to meet while supporting various community groups through volunteering.

"Because we have one thing in common, being single, it benefits our members as we immediately all have something in common," says Debbie Kean, president.

If you are seeking to grow your volunteer numbers, learn from the successes of Volunteer Singles. Kean shares strategies that have made Single Volunteers of Northeast Ohio one of the most sought after membership organizations by singles:

❑ *Make members feel comfortable and welcome at all events, particularly meetings.* If new members or volunteers have fun at an event and — if they have been made to feel comfortable — they will be telling friends about Single Volunteers. Follow these ways to encourage socializing and fun at meetings:
  • Engage attendees in ice-breaker games.
  • Assigning greeters at each meeting to sign in attendees as they enter the meeting. Greeters also shake their hand and tell them about the group.
  • Enlist officers to go from table to table during the meeting, introducing themselves to new attendees.

❑ *Offer volunteer activities and events that naturally attract singles.* While service is the key to this organization, social gatherings are also promoted on the nonprofit's website. Under the Cleveland Events tab of the website, one can find mention of summer dances and rib cook-offs intermingled with volunteer events. The blend makes it easy for singles to mix and mingle as well as lend a hand.

❑ *Involve board members.* At monthly meetings board members are asked to sit at a different table which allows new attendees to have an opportunity to ask questions about the membership group. These board members are also the biggest advocates of the group and are not shy about talking-up Single Volunteers.

❑ *Assign a social greeter.* Single Volunteers also assigns a point of contact at each event whose job it is to coordinate the event as well as to make each person feel welcome.

❑ *Heavily promote the organization's website and purpose.* This organization's website at www.svohio. org is advertised in local newspapers, as well as social networks, and feedback indicates that those publications are, in fact, getting the word out.

Source: Debbie Kean, President, Single Volunteers of Northeast Ohio, Olmsted Falls, OH. Phone (216) 534-7024. E-mail: singlevolunteers.cleveland@yahoo.com. Website: www.svohio.org

Attract Single Working Parents as Volunteers

Single working parents may wish to participate more actively in volunteer activities, but feel unable to do so because of family and career responsibilities. Take their special circumstances into consideration by using techniques such as these to provide opportunities for single working parents to help your cause:

1. **Recruit teen volunteers to baby-sit younger children.** Develop a group of youth who are old enough to baby-sit children during meetings. Reward them with certificates or recognition. Not only will they become familiar with your organization at an early age, but parents can attend to business knowing that responsible youth are nearby caring for and entertaining their little ones.

2. **Give volunteers some supplies for a home office.** Some volunteers may have time to offer once they have fed, bathed and put their children to bed. Later evening hours may be the best time for them to accomplish their tasks.

3. **Offer them jobs that involve their children.** When you need signs or posters created, envelopes stuffed or other routine but crucial tasks completed, see if the parent of an elementary or junior high-age child wants the task. Older children may be eager to help paint, draw, sort mailings and accomplish other simple duties. Remember how easily children can turn work into fun. Many also are proficient with computers.

4. **Keep meeting attendance requirements reasonable.** While many volunteer organizations have fairly strong attendance requirements, think of important jobs that don't require a great deal of committee interaction so the parent won't have concerns about arrangements. Two or three times a year, plan a meeting that is casual enough or in a location that children may attend without disrupting business, such as in a facility with a gymnasium where children can play supervised games while parents meet nearby.

5. **Provide plenty of valuable contact with a knowledgeable liaison.** When an experienced committee chairperson or liaison can keep single parents updated on important developments, or agrees to be available as a mentor for that volunteer, fewer meetings are likely to be necessary.

6. **Develop a "Grandparent" team to spend time with children.** Many senior citizens' facilities have started grandparent programs with small children in churches or other organizations, see if older volunteers would like to have a story time or special activity with the children of your single volunteers that coincides with your group meetings.

7. **Write a press release about how you are helping single parents volunteer.** Once you have two or three plans established to accommodate single parents while they complete their assignments, write a press release telling media what those plans are and how they work. Those waiting for an opportunity to volunteer will be made aware of your efforts, and positive publicity may encourage wider media interest.

Recruit Couples to Volunteer

Do you have volunteer projects that reach out to couples?

Inviting couples to volunteer gives them the opportunity to be together as they serve a common effort, offers a ready-made comfort level of working with a familiar face and strengthens their relationship.

You benefit by getting two volunteers with each request instead of one.

To initiate a program that encourages couples to volunteer:

1. **Identify volunteer opportunities that most appeal to couples.** Survey employees to identify couples' opportunities. Create a checklist of projects ranging from simple to complex — filing, staffing front desk, co-chairing an event, team phoning or solicitation, serving as hosts guiding tour, etc.

2. **Develop a plan to market volunteer projects to couples.** Consider an ad program that reaches out to couples and lists volunteer opportunities. Recruit a couple to head up your couples' program and enlist others. Do a feature story on a volunteer couple to illustrate the rewards of couples volunteering.

3. **Work with couples to keep them invigorated.** Once you have couples involved, find out which projects they find most rewarding and weed out those they do not. Ask couples what can be done to support their work.

4. **Identify unique ways to recognize couples' efforts.** Host periodic appreciation events for all volunteering couples. Offer special bus trips or discounts to restaurants. Make volunteering as a couple attractive to those who have not yet stepped forward.

PROCEDURES FOR RECRUITING QUALITY VOLUNTEERS

Implement Strategies That Reach Out to Minorities

If your organization is seeking to gain greater support from minorities in your area — whether it is their time, services or financial support — there are a number of points and possible approaches to consider before you begin.

Begin by identifying the specific minority groups you want to reach. Do some of your programs and services benefit these people? Have any aspects of your mission changed to better serve their needs? If so, might they be willing and able to become volunteers when they no longer require assistance?

Try these strategies to enlist help from minority groups, and build your organization's track record of successful programs that fill a variety of community needs:

- **Read publications produced by minority groups.** Depending on the size of your city, there may be many newspapers, magazines, newsletters or even television and radio programs that will help you become familiar with specific concerns or needs that may exist. Explore possible mutually beneficial relationships between members of your target minority group and use of your programs.

- **Seek out successful persons for their input.** Every group of individuals who share a cultural background has leaders and spokespersons, many of whom are successful in business or civic roles. Ask them to help your organization in long-range planning to better serve minority youth, families or seniors.

- **Determine the varying degrees of need.** As in every population, there will be persons who are successful and prosperous, middle income or in need of assistance. Seek a balance of involvement among them. The success and experiences of those who are able to contribute can inspire those who are receiving, and promote an atmosphere of dignity and cooperation for the entire organization.

- **Plan events that will be attractive to different cultures.** If your community has a significant population of a minority group, create festivals or other types of events that appeal to them. Ask minority leaders to help you with authenticity and accuracy — make the event a true celebration of diversity to appeal to all of your supporters.

- **Recognize the valuable perspective minorities can offer.** Remember that the world is getting smaller — we now speak of a global economy and overseas markets in business. The same applies to charitable organizations; if you are to grow and thrive, multicultural input will be essential to your growth and success.

Volunteer Informational Sessions Help Educate, Recruit

Whet potential volunteers' appetites with an upbeat, brief informational session about helping your cause.

Five years ago, the Vanderbilt University Medical Center (Nashville, TN) began offering volunteer information sessions as a starting point for some of its 650 existing volunteers as well as persons interested in volunteering at the Monroe Carell Jr. Children's Hospital at Vanderbilt, Vanderbilt Medical Center and Vanderbilt Health – One Hundred Oaks, says Stephanie VanDyke, director of volunteer services at Monroe Carell Jr. Children's Hospital at Vanderbilt.

VanDyke says the sessions showcase hospital values, expectations and specific volunteer openings. In addition, they help educate potential volunteers about duties and expectations, and reduce costs for volunteer training by helping match recruits to appropriate volunteer tasks.

The training sessions feature a 15-minute video with interviews from current volunteers, an overview of the hospital and a look at the commitment and training that goes with being a hospital volunteer.

The one-hour sessions are offered one evening a month in January, March, May, August and September. VanDyke and Andrew Peterson, director of volunteer services at the adult hospital and clinics, say they see the highest attendance in August and September because many college students are available then. January is also another popular month because many people sign up to volunteer during the holiday season.

Interested volunteers are required to attend the informational sessions and must register in advance. Peterson says they advertise the informational sessions on the Vanderbilt website about four weeks before the session date. Posting the information any earlier, he says, can result in many people signing up, but then forgetting or losing interest. He adds that they have found that directing people to their website is the best way to advertise an upcoming session.

After the session, the attendees are given the opportunity to sign up for an interview, with about 90 percent of them doing so. Once the interview is complete, Vanderbilt works to have the new recruits in place within three to four weeks.

With the large number of interested volunteers, space limitations and the ability to follow-up and schedule interviews in a 3-to 4-week time frame, organizers limit the number of attendees at each session. On average Vanderbilt has 50 to 60 people register for each session.

Sources: Andrew Peterson, Director of Volunteer Services, Vanderbilt Medical Center, Nashville, TN. Phone (615) 936-8871. E-mail: andrew.r.peterson@Vanderbilt.Edu
Stephanie VanDyke, Director, Volunteer Services, Monroe Carell Jr. Children's Hospital at Vanderbilt, Nashville, TN.
Phone (615) 343-3692. E-mail:stephanie.vandyke@Vanderbilt.Edu
Website: http://childrenshospital.vanderbilt.org/

Forms — Both Pre-filled and Blank — 'Sell' Volunteer Slots

Online volunteer recruitment forms can encourage new and existing members and volunteers to share their expertise within your organization.

The Technical Association of the Pulp and Paper Industry (TAPPI) of Norcross, GA, accomplishes this through two new volunteer recruitment forms on its website that encourage more members — new and existing — to volunteer within the TAPPI ranks.

Serving more than 20,000 professionals in the paper, packaging and converting industry, TAPPI is currently testing the forms intended to encourage volunteer participation among members and identify skill levels as well as need within the TAPPI community, says Rich Lapin, marketing manager.

Lapin explains the purpose of the new forms:

Blank volunteer form (top right): This open-ended request to members allows potential volunteers to raise their hand to become involved, Lapin says. Areas such as experience level, location and division/committee are intentionally left blank for volunteers to complete. The form offers those new to the industry and recent college graduates the opportunity to participate readily within the organization by offering their new skills through volunteerism.

The form is also intended for use by division and committee leaders as a resource to identify current volunteer needs within their division and to place volunteers based on experience and skill levels within the organization. Once a potential volunteer completes this form, committee leaders review it to determine where the person may best fit within the volunteer realm of the organization.

Completed volunteer form (lower right): This form is intended to "sell" specific volunteer opportunities within the organization by offering detailed descriptions of volunteer posts. The form also guides division and committee leaders as they prepare for immediate volunteer needs. These detailed volunteer descriptions include specifics such as division/committee, volunteer title, number of positions available, time commitment, project type, experience level needed, job description and benefits for participating.

Most importantly, Lapin says, this form offers a posting date for the opportunity as well as a posting expiration date. A posting date indicates when the position first becomes available and the expiration date is tied to the term of service needed. This allows volunteer coordinating staff to track when a position completes its term of service or the time by which a new volunteer is needed for that office.

Source: Rich Lapin, Marketing Manager, Technical Association of the Pulp and Paper Industry, Norcross, GA. Phone (770) 209-7290. E-mail: rlapin@tappi.org. Website: www.tappi.org

Content not available in this edition

Content not available in this edition

Useful Policies, Examples and Forms for the Volunteer Manager

SCREENING, ORIENTATION AND TRAINING TOOLS

Important as it may be, recruitment is only the first of many steps in the volunteer/nonprofit relationship. Advancing that relationship involves screening volunteers for potential red flags, orienting them to the organization in which they will be working and training them in the procedures they will be expected to master. To help your organization tend to these important tasks, consult the experience-tested methods and approaches outlined below.

Require and Check Volunteer References to Protect Organization, Reduce Headaches

If your volunteer application doesn't include a request for references, it should.

Asking volunteer applicants for names and contact information for persons to whom they are not related — and then touching base with those references — can prevent you from signing on a volunteer who could wreak havoc in your nonprofit.

Ask each new volunteer for at least three references and then call each one before assigning a volunteer position. Take notes about what you're told and look for inconsistencies among the information you're given by each reference. Treat your volunteer applicant as though he/she is applying for a new paid position within your nonprofit. Ask the same questions of references as you would if this were a new hire, and include notes of your conversations in the volunteer file.

If an applicant gets a negative review from one or more references, weigh your options carefully. Try the following:

- Simply decline the person's application and offer feedback based on your reference check.

- Fill the applicant in on anything negative that may have been mentioned during the reference review and ask that the volunteer address each item raised. If you're satisfied with the volunteer's response, invite him/her to join your nonprofit in a probationary fashion.

- Ask the volunteer to help at a one-time event. Monitor that person closely during the event, and if things go well, invite them to help out until a positive history is proven.

Know that reference checks are just one step in the volunteer applicant assessment process. Be sure to require background checks and other specific screenings to best protect your organization and those you serve.

Combine Background Checks to Save Time, Funds

Consider working with another volunteer organization to conduct volunteer background checks to save on costs and resources.

The Kalamazoo Valley Museum (Kalamazoo, MI) requires background checks on all of its volunteers as many work with young children who visit the museum to take part in the many educational opportunities offered there. The museum, operated by the Kalamazoo Valley Community College (Kalamazoo, MI), seeks to develop cultural, historical and scientific literacy through innovative exhibits, special exhibitions, planetarium programs, educational programs and family events.

Working with the community college that operates the museum, all museum volunteers undergo a criminal background check prior to taking on duties.

The organizations use the same consent form, which saves on costs and clears persons who pass the criminal record checks to volunteer for the museum, college or both.

Source: Annette Hoppenworth, Programs Coordinator, Kalamazoo Valley Museum, Kalamazoo, MI and Kalamazoo Valley Community College, Kalamazoo, MI. Phone (269) 373-7997. E-mail: ahoppenworth@kvcc.edu. Website: www.kvm.kvcc.edu

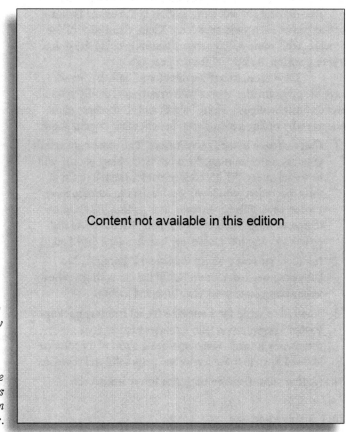

Content not available in this edition

Potential volunteers at the Kalamazoo Valley Community College and Kalamazoo Valley Museum (both of Kalamazoo, MI), fill out this consent form, which allows officials at the organizations to perform a criminal record check before assigning them volunteer tasks.

Plan for Following Up on Background Check Rejection

If you require candidates to pass a background check before becoming volunteers, consider creating a plan for those volunteers who do not clear the background check.

Background checks can identify criminal behavior, evaluate for drug usage or check financial references. Due to data privacy protection laws, you may not learn the specific reason someone is being declined in a background check. Therefore, you will want to put into practice a system for dealing with those who are rejected.

Consider the following:

- Will your nonprofit eliminate all volunteer prospects that do not pass a background check? If so, create a form letter or dialogue that explains to candidates the reason behind the rejection of their volunteer assistance and provide them with the name of the entity that provided the background check. This will allow persons to follow up and clear discrepancies, if applicable.

- Taking into consideration the constituents you serve, would reassigning rejected volunteers to a monitored volunteer effort not dealing directly with constituents be fruitful for your nonprofit? Could these volunteers work on mailings or other supervised administrative tasks that do not directly influence vulnerable clients?

- Should you ask applicants to clear discrepancies and resubmit their application after another check is conducted and cleared?

Making a plan to handle rejected volunteer background checks will create a course of action that reflects the professionalism of your nonprofit and may allow you to utilize all volunteers who apply.

One last thought: If it's necessary to perform background checks on your applicant volunteers, you may consider signing on with a professional background screening service. Check with other nonprofits in your region for recommendations of exceptional screening services or check the National Association of Professional Background Screeners at www.napbs.com to find a list of screeners serving your area.

Eight Benefits to Training Volunteers Online

Is an online training option right for your volunteers?

For three years, the Catholic Diocese of Sioux Falls (Sioux Falls, SD) has used a Web-based version of the Safe & Sacred Environment training program (Minneapolis, MN), which focuses on training for volunteers who interact with children.

Recruitment for and participation in the online training option grows each year, says Jerry Klein, chancellor of the diocese, with some 4,000 persons currently using the online training option, up by 500 from a year ago.

DJ Paxton, executive director of Safe & Sacred, says the program also works with preschools, public schools and technical colleges. Here, Paxton and Klein share eight reasons why online training may benefit other organizations:

1. **Convenience boosts recruitment.** The more convenient you can make training, the more likely busy people will be to volunteer. "If it's convenient for them to train at their discretion, you lower the barriers to participation," Paxton says. "They can train after putting the children to bed or while waiting for a flight." Klein attests that online training has closed any training gaps they had.

2. **It shows you care about volunteers' finances.** No babysitter needed, no need to fill the car with gas, shows volunteers you respect their time and money.

3. **No need to settle for a one-size-fits-all training package.** Paxton's organization tailors courses to meet each community's needs. Klein says being a part of the training allowed them to make it relevant, purposeful and relatable.

4. **Online volunteer training can lower insurance costs.** When volunteers work with children, it's almost a guarantee that you have to be insured by a risk management company, says Paxton. That company may provide financial incentives for providing such training.

5. **You can recruit from far and wide.** Unlike in-person training, online training does not limit your recruitment reach or require a physical meeting space.

6. **A prospective volunteer can begin working with your group at any time.** With no need to wait for a training session, an eager volunteer-to-be can hit the ground running. "You don't want to ever tell a volunteer, 'No, you can't start working for us yet,'" says Paxton. "With online training, someone who's eager can go home, do the training tonight, then come back tomorrow."

7. **You can still offer face-to-face training.** As part of its package, Safe & Sacred offers the training in book format, says Paxton, "for people who aren't comfortable using computers."

8. **Your staff won't be as stretched.** Who runs your volunteer training now? Is it a management person who has many other hats to wear? "Some of our clients like that they're giving work hours back to their paid staff members who can then use that time to focus on fundraising or other aspects," says Paxton.

Sources: Jerry Klein, Chancellor, Catholic Diocese of Sioux Falls, Sioux Falls, SD. Phone (605) 334-9861. E-mail: jklein@sfcatholic.org DJ Paxton, Executive Director, Safe & Sacred Environment Training Program, Minneapolis, MN. Phone (612) 216-4988. E-mail:dj@safeenvironmenttraining.com

Create 'No Frills' Training, Opportunities for Busy Volunteers

In today's on-the-go society, time is tight for many people. Their jobs demand most of their attention; they're working and raising families; they're multitasking throughout their day; often, they are very driven personalities.

Yet, many such people may be willing to volunteer if able to do so on their own time and terms.

How can you accommodate these individuals who want to make a meaningful contribution and then get on with their lives? How can you convince them that you will meet them on their terms? Try these proven methods:

- Develop a menu of specific tasks from which they can choose that include brief job descriptions and the time estimated to complete each duty.

- Avoid offering volunteer jobs in which outside factors — setting appointments with others, tasks that involve waiting — may impede the timely completion of their responsibilities.

- Eliminate any frills — socializing, waiting for others to arrive, etc. — that prevent these volunteers from starting and finishing projects on their time.

- Make training time efficient. Consider sending training material in advance to avoid using on-the-job time for that purpose.

- Provide them with multiple choices of times in which to show up and complete tasks.

- Err on the side of protecting their time. If, for instance, a task has not yet been fully completed by the time the volunteer said he/she would need to leave, have another volunteer prepared to step in and complete it for him/her.

Chances are good that you can keep these no-frills volunteers coming back if you can accommodate their demands early on in your relationship with them. Although each volunteer commitment may be a brief in-and-out experience — or even involve their working from home — they will come to claim your organization as their own in time.

Offer Online Orientation, Other Web-based Resources

If your volunteer-driven organization is part of a national group, contact your national headquarters today to determine if online orientation or other volunteer training tools are available to post at your chapter's website.

If you're not associated with a national organization, consider creating an online orientation to present the mission of your nonprofit to interested volunteers.

Offering online orientation not only conserves staff time, but can also offer volunteers a window on the organization, helping them to determine if your organization is right for them.

Officials with the Northern Colorado American Red Cross Chapter (Fort Collins, CO) have found a fast, effective way to orientate volunteers with an online orientation. They use this online training as a prerequisite to formal training offered onsite at the Red Cross chapter.

According to Sarah Bray, volunteer program coordinator, the online orientation is one of the many benefits of being associated with a national organization. Effective tools are developed and orchestrated by the national organization. Individual chapters are then able to access those tools for online training.

"Our chapter recommends that our volunteers take both online courses before attending our two-hour new volunteer orientation offered at our chapter headquarters where the potential new volunteers hear stories from current volunteers and staff members as they take a walking tour of our facility," says Bray. "We find that the combination of the online orientation and the walking tour helps the potential volunteer learn more about the organization and also gives us the opportunity to meet and visit with the new volunteer before they start their journey as a volunteer."

The online orientation is broken into a series of four audio and slide modules, takes 70 minutes for a volunteer to complete and includes the topics: history, foundations, key services and commitments.

Find this online orientation at www.northerncolorado. redcross.org/Volunteer.

Source: Sarah Bray, Volunteer Program Coordinator, American Red Cross Northern Colorado Chapter, Fort Collins, CO. Phone (970) 226-5728. E-mail: brays@CentennialArc.org. Website: www.northerncolorado.redcross.org

Streamline Processes to Accommodate Professionals

Staff and volunteers at HealthFinders (Northfield, MN) provide healthcare to underserved residents in Rice County, MN. Providing 700 free clinic visits a year while serving low-income residents requires volunteer efforts of medical professionals.

Because these volunteers lead full professional lives in addition to their volunteer commitment at HealthFinders, clinic staff developed a streamlined, condensed training process and highly effective communication, says Angelica Koch, director of HealthFinders.

"We've really come to know our volunteers and the level of communication they need to feel in control of their volunteer efforts, especially when it is so sporadic," says Koch. "It's vitally important to not overload volunteer professionals, but also give them enough information to understand the process and not feel lost."

Koch shares tips for working with busy volunteer professionals:

❑ **Establish fluid lines of communication with professionals.** This includes ongoing e-mail and phone calls to providers before volunteering regarding special cases;

communication after volunteering in case of needed follow-up; and, updates and presentations in the provider meetings at their own clinic sites.

❑ **Back up e-mail communications with hard copies.** Busy medical professionals need the reinforcement of hardcopy documentation to ensure that e-mails are not overlooked or missed.

❑ **Offer at least one tidbit of technical information within the newsletter each month that will aide volunteer professionals in their work.**

❑ **Provide volunteer professionals with an expedited version of your formal training to accommodate their schedules.** HealthFinders revamped their training process to prioritize the most critical information and condense the time it takes for training.

❑ **Have at least one regular staffer per shift as the go-to person for questions about standard operating procedure.**

Source: Angelica Koch, Director, HealthFinders, Northfield, MN. Phone (507) 330-4031. E-mail: koch.angelica@healthfindersmn.org. Website: www.healthfindersmn.org

Create Interactive Seminars to Engage, Energize Volunteers

Don't offer the same old, same old when it comes to your annual volunteer training or new volunteer orientation. Instead, look for interactive opportunities at your seminars to engage and energize your volunteers while leaving them more likely to remember the important lessons learned.

That's what officials with Women On the Move (Boynton Beach, FL) and the KARS Consulting Group (Boynton Beach, FL) accomplished in summer 2010 when they collaborated to create a seminar tour to assist women-run and women-focused nonprofits, organizations and businesses in the art of grant writing.

The hands-on interactive seminar series teaches attendees how to create effective, compelling grant proposals and explore methods to garner support for their organization and ensure sustainability through the acquisition of volunteers, donations, fundraising and sponsorships.

To keep participants actively engaged during the seminar, event organizers implemented the following to create an interactive environment:

✓ Teams prepared elevator pitches to give to the class, which helped them with their presentations skills and ensured the audience's attention.

✓ Mock videos were created and presented to the class to keep the audience engaged.

✓ Abbreviated grant proposals were constructed by the teams and presented to show the audience how to proceed with this process.

✓ Individual interviews were conducted. Class participants interviewed each other which kept discussions lively.

✓ Teams evaluated one another.

Source: Leslie Harris, Women On the Move, Inc., Boynton Beach, FL. Phone (561) 200-0580. E-mail: info@mywomenonthemove.com. Website: www.mywomenonthemove.com

Varying Teaching Styles Offers Well-rounded Training

Consider using multiple teaching styles to help volunteers-in-training remain engaged and retain more of the important information they need to assist your organization and its mission.

At Fox Valley Volunteer Hospice (FVVH) of Geneva, IL, persons can expect a variety of teaching styles during their training sessions to help them prepare as thoroughly as possible for the often-emotional tasks involved with volunteering at the organization.

Training as an FVVH bereavement volunteer requires more than 20 hours of intensive training to learn the unique aspects of serving and supporting individuals and families who have experienced the death of a loved one, says Elise C. Wall, manager of volunteer services. Bereavement volunteers not only need to have compassion, Wall says, they need to learn skills in discussing grief, death and dying; to listen without judgment; and to maintain personal boundaries.

Topics covered during training at FVVH include normal adult and children's grief, complicated grief, good communication skills with an emphasis on listening, self-care for both client and volunteer, exploring grief theories and preventing volunteer burnout.

To best cover this extensive list of complicated topics, Wall says, bereavement training includes a variety of teaching and learning styles to assist new volunteers with retention as follows:

❑ **Lectures.** Lectures can offer thorough details and explanations to volunteers, but can also be an area where volunteers lose information when their minds become inundated or overloaded. Be sure to break lecture training up with frequent breaks as well as small-group discussions and role-playing. Create handouts with bullet points of critical information that will allow volunteers the opportunity to review material covered.

❑ **Small-group discussions.** Break volunteers into small groups of five or fewer to review accompanying lecture materials or to personalize the information covered based on their experiences, as part of the layering process that will help them retain information.

❑ **Role playing.** Offer role-playing to allow volunteers to put the training into action and affirm what they have learned. Ask trainers and seasoned volunteers to role-play with trainees to ensure their understanding of material covered.

❑ **Onsite training.** Create opportunities for new volunteers to put their new knowledge into play within your organization by offering onsite training. Either pair new volunteers together or ask them to shadow experienced volunteers to witness training techniques in action.

Source: Elise C. Wall, Manager of Volunteer Services, Fox Valley Volunteer Hospice, Geneva, IL. Phone (630) 232-2233. E-mail: ewall@fvvh.org. Website: www.fvvh.org

---

Teach Art of Effective Listening

A key component to offering effective support to clients facing the death of a loved one is the art of effective listening. In bereavement training, volunteers at the Fox Valley Volunteer Hospice (Geneva, IL) learn to listen effectively.

Elise C. Wall, manager of volunteer services, shares techniques they use, which can also help your volunteers to become more effective listeners:

✓ Listening with the intent to understand rather than with the intent to respond.

✓ Using open body language (e.g. arms and legs uncrossed).

✓ Maintaining eye contact with the client.

✓ Staying focused on the client, not allowing the mind to wander.

✓ Affirming the client's words with a nod.

✓ Being comfortable with silence, allowing the client to process his/her thoughts.

✓ Avoiding jumping to conclusions.

Useful Policies, Examples and Forms for the Volunteer Manager

CLARIFYING VOLUNTEER ROLES AND RESPONSIBILITIES

How many businesses would think of trying to fill a paid position with no description of the duties and responsibilities involved? And yet countless nonprofits ask volunteers to report for their first day of work with no formal description of the tasks they will be expected to perform. Get your new volunteers started off right by employing the following advice on ways to clarify volunteer roles and responsibilities.

Dos and Don'ts for Defining Volunteer Roles

Creating a volunteer job description is the first step for assigning the correct person to any volunteer role. Recruiting volunteers under the general volunteer label can lump too many individuals with varied backgrounds and skills into the same generic category.

Gather your volunteer management staff and ask the questions, "What do we want this volunteer to do?" and "Where is our greatest need?" These questions will help you define volunteer roles within your nonprofit.

Follow this list of dos and don'ts when assigning volunteer job descriptions:

❑ Do set aside time with your management team to define volunteer objectives and specific roles.

❑ Don't take the task of setting volunteer roles lightly. Volunteers bring a breadth of skills and services to your organization, so it's important to treat this task as critical to your nonprofit.

❑ Do create a list of volunteer roles including a task sheet that details specific expectations about the role for the volunteer.

❑ Don't create a list of impossible expectations. Be realistic about the time allotted for each volunteer role and ensure that the expectations of the role fit the time frame. Creating an extensive list for a 10-hour-per-month volunteer role will only ensure a feeling of failure by the volunteer.

❑ Do list the skills the volunteer will need to successfully fulfill the role. Are computer skills, people skills or technological skills needed? If so, be sure to include as much detail about the required skill set as possible to avoid assigning the wrong volunteer to the role.

❑ Don't ask the volunteers to take on the slush pile of work that staff refuse to do. Expecting a volunteer to take on the least appealing work is a recipe for disaster.

❑ Do review the volunteer job descriptions to ensure that what was deemed important by your volunteer management staff is reflected in the job descriptions. Also, ask current volunteers to review the volunteer job descriptions and offer their feedback.

Think Through New Positions Before Filling Them

It's not uncommon to see a need that could be addressed by a volunteer and someone recruited for the task, only to find that something's not working. Perhaps the volunteer's interests or qualifications didn't meet the job's requirements, or the task involved a good deal more red tape than originally anticipated, or any number of other obstacles became road blocks to success.

To keep this from happening to you, it's important to have a procedure in place whenever you — or other employees — want to create a new volunteer task or project.

To help think new projects through before recruiting volunteers to assist, address certain basic issues that will help determine the type and number of volunteers needed, the length of time that the project or task will run, the hours, etc.

The new project summary form (at right) is one tool that will help during this start-up phase. By completing the form and discussing it with those who will be involved with subsequent decisions can be made in a more enlightened way, resulting in an effectively managed project.

NEW PROJECT SUMMARY

Project or task purpose _____
_____

No. of volunteers required ____ Volunteer(s) responsible to _____

Nature of volunteer work _____

Project duration: Beginning _____ Ending _____

Days and/or hours _____
_____

Volunteer qualifications_____

Volunteer benefits _____
_____

Benefits to organization _____
_____
_____

CLARIFYING VOLUNTEER ROLES AND RESPONSIBILITIES

Create Volunteer Manual to Streamline Process

Use your organization's staff manual as a basis from which to create one for volunteers.

"Our volunteer manual upholds the same expectations in terms of health and safety with the volunteers as the staff in the staff manual," says Becky Carlino, director of community engagement at the Western Reserve Historical Society (Cleveland, OH). "The volunteer handbook is an essential part of a fully functioning volunteer program. It provides clear guidelines with regard to expectations for work, relationships between volunteers and staff, and the rights and responsibilities of volunteers and staff when working together."

Working in tandem with the Forum for Volunteer Administrators (Cleveland, OH) — an organization ensuring that similar organizations in the region follow the same protocol — Carlino organized her volunteer manual with the following headings (which may work for other nonprofits):

- History and About the Organization — including staff structure.
- Mission and Vision of the Organization.
- Volunteer Program Structure outlining who reports to whom.
- Volunteer Policy — topics include: Involvement, Service, Management Rights, Membership, Youth, Background Investigations, Training, Attendance, Dress Code, Conduct, Placement, Computer Use Policy.
- Company and Volunteer Policies — topics include: EEO Statement, Intellectual Property, Media, Telephone Usage.

- Company Safety Policy — topics include: Unsafe Working Conditions, Safety Training, Drug Free Workplace, Smoking Policy, Violence in the Workplace, Visitors in Work Areas, No Weapons Policy.
- State and Federal Laws Regarding Volunteerism.
- Acknowledgement of Receipt and Volunteer's Copy of Acknowledgement form.

Source: Becky Carlino, Director of Community Engagement, Western Reserve Historical Society, Cleveland, OH. Phone (216) 721-5722. E-mail: bcarlino@wrhs.org. Website: www.wrhs.org

Create Reference Manual From Menu of Topics

If you plan to create a volunteer reference manual or evaluate your existing manual, consider these topics for inclusion, then involve one or two existing volunteers to determine what topics to include to create a more user-friendly resource:
- ❑ Mission statement
- ❑ Historical information
- ❑ Bylaws
- ❑ Policy statements/summaries
- ❑ Annual goals
- ❑ Strategic plan summary
- ❑ Organizational structure
- ❑ Volunteer structure
- ❑ List of phone number
- ❑ Volunteer job descriptions
- ❑ Volunteer opportunities
- ❑ Code of volunteer ethics
- ❑ Confidentiality statement
- ❑ Rules and regulations
- ❑ How-to information
- ❑ Volunteer agreement form

Provide Guidelines for Your Employee Volunteers

When employees wish to volunteer within your organization, should they have to follow specific guidelines to do so? Absolutely, says Alfreda Rooks, director of volunteer services at the University of Michigan Health System (UMHS), Ann Arbor, MI. "Having guidelines insures that the employee is aware that there are boundaries between being an employee and being a volunteer.

"We have a clearly defined code of conduct and behavior expectations for all volunteers, including those volunteers who are employed by UMHS," says Rooks. "The guidelines help to avoid any possible conflicts that may arise before they happen."

Every volunteer must complete a volunteer application, provide two written references and undergo a background check.

"Because criminal history background checks currently only occur when you are a new hire, the director of security recommends that employees who volunteer be screened the same as current volunteers," says Rooks. Since employees undergo a yearly health screening, they do not need to do the new volunteer health screening.

Typically, employees wishing to volunteer at the hospital come from clerical or other support positions, Rooks says.

And while many employees choose to volunteer in an effort to change their career or get experience, Rooks says there are issues to consider when having employees volunteer. "Employees wishing to volunteer in traditional volunteer roles, for example, on patient floors are discouraged from volunteering in the same role for which they are paid. We would discourage a nurse from volunteering in a clinical/nursing support role."

On average, the medical facility has more than 1,600 volunteers on hand. For persons currently employed with the health system, there is a special link on the UMHS Volunteer Services website stating the guidelines.

Says Rooks, "Guidelines serve as a reminder to the employee that during the time they volunteer, their behavior cannot be that of an employee, for example, offering suggestions, services, etc. Nor can they function in their employee role. This protects the patients they come in contact with and the employee in their volunteer role."

Source: Alfreda R. Rooks, Director of Volunteer Services, University of Michigan Health System. Ann Arbor, MI. E-mail: arooks@umich.edu. Phone (734) 936-4327. Website: http://www.med.umich.edu/volunteer

Proceed Slowly With Online Volunteer Descriptions

Becky Ricketts, community resource manager for SeniorCare Experts (Louisville, KY), says she grappled with the decision to post volunteer job descriptions on the organization's website.

Ricketts says she hesitated because of concern that including too much detail about volunteer roles could backfire, turning prospects away. So the organization first tested the idea to evaluate its effectiveness. The result is a website that is constantly being evaluated, and which currently features volunteer job descriptions for key positions, with duties described in encouraging terms.

If you haven't taken the leap to add volunteer job descriptions to your website, Ricketts suggests following these ideas for testing the concept:

❑ Consider only adding staple positions. Ricketts has decided to add only key volunteer position descriptions such as board member, meal delivery person and transport drivers at the site to test this approach to recruitment.

❑ Add key phrases on the volunteer description page to encourage volunteerism such as "Volunteering makes you happier!" or "Volunteering keeps you active and healthy."

❑ Track response from your Web page by asking applicants where they heard about volunteer posts. Evaluate responses monthly or quarterly to determine how posting job descriptions promotes volunteerism at your nonprofit.

❑ Ask new applicants who are responding to postings at your website pointed questions about the effectiveness of this idea. Obtain information from new volunteers to address issues or concerns about the clarity of the information posted and tweak as needed.

Source: Becky Ricketts, Community Resource Manager, SeniorCare Experts, Louisville, KY. Phone (502) 896-2316.
E-mail: b.ricketts@srcareexperts.org.
Website: www.srcareexperts.org

Checklist Helps in Crafting a New Volunteer Position

Have you come to the conclusion that your organization could justify creating a new volunteer position?

If so, do your homework before asking your supervisors to approve the new position or recruiting volunteers to fill it.

Follow a planning checklist that ensures the new position has been well thought through, to reassure your superiors of its need and value, and to enable new recruits to hit the ground running when they assume their duties.

A checklist such as the one shown here will help you justify the position and plan for its effective implementation.

New Position Checklist

❑ Job description
❑ Qualifications of position
❑ Training required
❑ Anticipated budget needs
❑ Project timeline
❑ Method of recruitment
❑ Method for evaluation
❑ Amount of staff support
❑ Methods for monitoring/supervising
❑ Areas of sensitivity/confidentiality
❑ Set hours/days per week
❑ Work is done on- or off-site
❑ Adequate workspace and conditions
❑ Description of goals/objectives
❑ Relationship of position to other volunteers/staff

Useful Policies, Examples and Forms for the Volunteer Manager

RESOURCES FOR ASSIGNING AND SCHEDULING VOLUNTEERS

Figuring out what person is best for what role, and what role is best for what person, lies at the heart of every effective volunteer program. Just as important is an organization's ability to effectively schedule its volunteers — making sure their time is used but not overused, creating a master schedule acceptable to all involved, etc. Mastering these critical issues will lay a foundation for success and put any volunteer program on firm and sustainable footing.

Confirm Volunteer Assignments in Writing

What tools do you provide your volunteers to help them succeed?

As you work with multiple volunteers on projects requiring their individualized follow-up, your odds of having them complete assigned tasks will improve significantly if you provide each volunteer with written confirmation of what it is he/she is supposed to do (and by when).

Whenever you conduct a meeting in which volunteers leave with agreed-to tasks, immediately send them a personalized memo — as opposed to a standardized group memo — confirming their duties. Spell out exactly what is expected of them, and be sure to include a deadline for the project (or multiple deadlines for portions of the project).

In addition to delineating each task, clearly state how to report back or turn in completed work. This helps bring closure to the task.

Here are two techniques you may want to include in your memo:

1. Offer an incentive for completing tasks on time.

2. Add a final sentence to your memo indicating that all persons not having completed their tasks by the stated deadline will be contacted by you (or the appropriate person) to determine what needs to happen in order to finish the project. Adding a closing statement such as this motivates volunteers to avoid the embarrassment of being contacted while, at the same time, provides you with a justifiable reason for following up with them.

January 3, 2011

St. Joseph's Hospital
FOUNDATION

TO: Tom Peterson, Sponsorship Committee
FROM: Brenda M. Hawley, Sponsorship Chairperson
RE: Calls to Be Completed By February 15
CC: Debra M. Brown, Director of Alumni

Thank you, Tom, for attending the December 13 Sponsorship Committee meeting and agreeing to call on the following businesses to serve as sponsors for our upcoming event.

As you know, it's imperative that we have commitments from these businesses by February 15 if we are to remain on schedule with our event timeline. For that reason, I am suggesting you schedule appointments for this week and next so business owners and managers have sufficient time to make a decision.

Please turn in (or fax) your completed calls to the Office of Alumni as you complete them. The fax number is 465-9097. As was mentioned at our meeting, those who turn in all calls on time will receive two 50 percent off coupons for dinner at Winchester's.

I encourage you to call me or Debra Brown if you have any questions, need any assistance or experience any difficulty that would impede your ability to complete these calls on schedule.

I will plan to contact any persons who have not turned in their calls to the Office of Alumni by February 15.

Thank you for your valuable assistance with this portion of our 2011 Celebrity Speaker Event.

<u>Sponsorship Calls to be Completed
by Tom Peterson by February 15:</u>

- Benders Office Supply & Equipment
- Determan Pepsi Distributors
- Osborne Trucking, Inc.
- Klein Brokers
- Castrole Travel
- Peterson Photography
- MasterCuts
- Winston Raceway

Detailed Online Graph Spells Out Volunteer Tasks

Clarify duties, expectations and anticipated time commitments for would-be volunteers to help them choose assignments that best match their interests and abilities.

View the volunteer opportunities chart for Friends of Filoli (Woodside, CA) at: www.filoli.org/volunteer/opportunities.html

More than 1,300 persons volunteer through The Friends of Filoli, a nonprofit charged with caring for the picturesque country estate, Filoli Center (Woodside, CA). The property is a historic site of the National Trust for Historic Preservation that features a stately home and 16-acre formal gardens.

To best match volunteers to job assignments, Carol Croce, vice president of volunteer resources, developed a detailed graph of available opportunities. The graph is broken into subsets of volunteering types and includes a description of the activity, attire needed, any prerequisite training and the level of commitment the assignment involves.

"The volunteer opportunities chart is posted on the website to educate potential volunteers about each committee before they complete an application for volunteering," Croce says. "They can choose which committees best meet their interests, skills and time commitment."

Croce shares the chart as a handout during twice-annual volunteer recruitment open houses, which she says helps the audience follow presentations by committee chairs outlining their committee's activities, time commitments and training requirements. "Most people mark up the chart with their questions for the chairs or circle those committees that are their top choices to join," she says. "This makes completing the volunteer application much easier for potential volunteers."

Having such a tool to help focus and explain volunteer duties is important for the organization, which currently has over 1,300 volunteers serving on 15 standing committees, Croce says. "All committees work year-round, though some are more active during the high visitor season from April to July. The committee model works well at Filoli, allowing volunteers to work within smaller groups focused on specific projects."

For organizations seeking to create a volunteer opportunities chart, Croce recommends:

✓ Working with committee chairs to clarify the descriptions for each part of the chart.

✓ Keeping the chart updated at least yearly so it reflects the correct time commitments and training requirements for each volunteer job listed.

✓ Spending time creating a detailed volunteer opportunities chart that not only features volunteer opportunities, but answers potential questions by volunteers.

Source: Carol Croce, Vice President of Volunteer Resources, Friends of Filoli, Woodside, CA. Phone (650) 364-8300. E-mail: volunteer@filoli.org. Website: www.filoli.org

Content not available in this edition

Discover Volunteers' Pet Peeves

So much emphasis is placed on learning about volunteers' interests and strengths that we often overlook their dislikes.

Knowing what irritates volunteers when they join your ranks will help you quell their possible frustrations.

Use various methods to help pull out pet peeves — brief surveys and one-on-one visits. Share a list of possible pet peeves to help them identify and prioritize their own.

You'll find that we can learn as much about people by knowing their dislikes as we can from their likes.

RESOURCES FOR ASSIGNING AND SCHEDULING VOLUNTEERS

Avoid Idle Time by Having Backup Checklist of Tasks

Secondary Projects List

___ Phone those who haven't ordered calendars.

___ Update volunteer bulletin board.

___ Write personalized thank-you notes.

___ Do an agency walk-through, noting signage (or lack thereof), cleanliness and other issues that should be addressed.

___ Update mailing list changes/additions.

___ File materials.

It's not healthy to have volunteers on hand with nothing to do. If they finish a task early, they'll get bored, and you'll miss out on getting some tasks accomplished.

Have a prioritized list of secondary projects or tasks available for volunteers if and when they finish a more important job. Having such a list available at all times helps avoid too much downtime for these dedicated individuals.

Plan Ahead for Successful Holiday Volunteer Effort

Finding persons to volunteer during the holidays requires pre-planning and organization.

The Bloch Cancer Hotline (Kansas City, MO) — a program of the R.A. Bloch Cancer Foundation — requires daily assistance of hotline volunteers. These volunteers must be knowledgeable and supportive of callers who are dealing with cancer, and be able to deal with the intense emotional conversations that can occur. Although call volume decreases during the holidays for this foundation's hotline service, each call can be more demanding because of the emotional toll cancer takes on patients during the holidays.

Rosanne Wickman, the foundation's hotline director, works to provide the same professional hotline service during the holidays as offered throughout the year. Wickman is mindful each year to plan for holiday volunteers who will need to fill in for regular volunteers who are not able to serve during the holiday season.

Knowing that there is a need for episodic volunteers this time of year, Wickman pre-plans to fill volunteer absences in the following ways:

✓ Recruits volunteers year-round who can substitute as needed. Wickman seeks volunteer assistance from local cancer survivors and often recruits at cancer-related fundraisers and events.

✓ Creates a master list of volunteers and maintains a sub-list of episodic and past volunteers to call for immediate assistance. The list includes the volunteer's contact e-mail and phone number so that contacting the volunteer is quick and easy.

✓ Creates a festive holiday environment with decorations and snacks to encourage volunteer retention and participation. Wickman also offers flexibility in start and end times as she schedules volunteers, remaining sensitive to the volunteer's personal needs during the holiday season and throughout the year.

✓ Creates a back-up system for substitute volunteers so they don't feel they're ill-equipped to handle callers' needs, making sure staff or seasoned volunteers are available to help episodic volunteers manage more demanding calls.

✓ Prepares staff for the possible need to fill in for volunteers over the holidays. She reminds staff that doing so is particularly important and that their extra efforts are appreciated and critical to the organization during the holiday season.

Source: Rosanne Wickman, Hotline Director, R.A. Bloch Cancer Foundation, Kansas City, MO. Phone (800) 433-0464. E-mail: rwickman@hrblock.com. Website: www.blochcancer.org

Online Tools Simplify Volunteer Scheduling Tasks

What if your volunteers could easily check their schedules, sign up for volunteer openings or receive an important message, all from their home computers?

Many companies offer volunteer management software designed to make the administrative process of volunteering simple. One such company — Volgistics (Grand Rapids, MI) — provides tools to help organizations track, manage and coordinate volunteers.

Volgistics' online volunteer portal, VicNet, allows volunteers access from anywhere they can log online. Once connected, volunteers view and manage their schedule, sign up for openings, update personal information, post hours and even check their service records. Organizations can send VIC Mail messages with important information for volunteers as well as post online volunteer applications.

Another Volgistics tool, VicTouch, is a touchscreen kiosk that volunteers can use at their volunteering site to sign in and out to automatically record their hours.

United Hospital (St. Paul, MN) has used VicNet and VicTouch for more than two years, says Heidi Nelsen, supervisor of volunteer and guest services, who notes that they find the software very user-friendly. "It's better for the volunteers, because they have the capability to schedule themselves from home. We also have it enabled in the system, so they can remove themselves from the schedule," Nelsen says. "We pretty much use VicNet for scheduling purposes at this point but are looking at ways to provide ongoing training materials as well."

She says the system has allowed the department to go paperless. "We no longer have paper applications or schedules," reducing both phone calls and paperwork.

The cost of this service depends on the number of volunteers the organization wants to track, the number of system operators and whether the customer uses VicNet or VicTouch. For example, an organization using VicNet to track up to 1,000 volunteers, 50 archived volunteers and two system operators will have a monthly fee of $53. For more information go to www.volgistics.com.

Sources: Volgistics Team, Grand Rapids, MI. E-mail: team@volgistics.com Website: www.volgistics.com
Heidi Nelsen, Supervisor, Volunteer & Guest Services, United Hospital, St. Paul, MN. Phone (651) 241-8605. E-mail: Heidi.Nelsen@allina.com

Implement a Skills-based Volunteer Program

In June 2010, officials with Little City Foundation (Palatine, IL) along with representatives of the Volunteer Center of Northwest Suburban Chicago (Chicago, IL) unveiled a new national model for executive-level volunteering.

At Little City Foundation — a human service agency serving persons with autism and other intellectual and developmental disabilities — implementing this type of volunteer program created valuable opportunities for executives in transition and afforded the opportunity to tap into the resources of skilled professionals, says Kathryn Nelson, volunteer manager.

Here, Nelson and Lisa Hoffmann, director of communications and marketing, share steps to implement a skills-based volunteer program at your nonprofit:

- First, gain your executive director's support to begin the program.

- Assign a volunteer manager or designate a lead volunteer to implement this program at your organization.

- Identify skills-based opportunities at your organization and create job descriptions (e.g., IT Support, Human Resources, Public Relations, etc.).

- Research volunteer programs in your area and introduce them to your organization's mission.

- Identify potential synergies with executives or professionals in transition with needs of your organization.

- Ask the skilled volunteers who have been identified if they would like to contribute their talents and skills to advance your agency's mission.

- Create a work plan with benchmarks and dates to promote and propel your mission with the help of skills-based volunteers.

- Engage volunteers immediately in a role that will match their talents with needs of your nonprofit.

Sources: Lisa Hoffmann, Director of Communications and Marketing, and Kathryn Nelson, Volunteer Manager, Little City Foundation, Palatine, IL. Phone (847) 358-5510.
E-mail: lhoffman@littlecity.org or knelson@littlecity.org.
Website: www.littlecity.org

Useful Policies, Examples and Forms for the Volunteer Manager

STRATEGIES FOR MANAGING VOLUNTEERS

Whether the issue be differences of opinion, contrasting expectations or outright conflict, managing others is an often-challenging proposition. It can be even more complicated in the context of volunteers who are freely giving of their time but could choose to stop at any moment. Building productive management practices that support supervisors and workers equally will go a long way towards stopping oversight trouble before it starts.

Strengthen Volunteer Corps Through Consensus Building

As a volunteer manager, one of your biggest goals may be getting key supporters to reach a meeting of the minds to achieve a common objective. This becomes even more difficult when two or more reasonable volunteers have differences of opinion on issues.

How can you help facilitate productive discussion when some of your most valued supporters disagree on how to reach a goal or approach a project?

Use these strategies to help diverse individuals find common ground:

- **Begin the planning process with clearly defined objectives.** When it's your role to bring a concept or proposal to your volunteers for consideration and eventual implementation, make it clear that everyone's initial input is important.

- **Involve your most likable volunteer leader or board member.** Because you want to stay on friendly terms with all of your volunteers, it may be helpful to call a meeting with your most respected and reasonable leader at the highest possible level. The fact that this individual is willing to spend time with your volunteers will make them feel valued and respected. He/she will know that an objective person who has the best interests of the majority at heart is carefully considering each differing idea.

- **Make a list of the pros and cons of each approach.** Ask each individual or group to list the advantages of their plan, as well as any obstacles they anticipate. You and key staff or volunteer officers can evaluate each one, then return to each party with your questions or concerns. Borrow the best ideas from both plans, emphasizing those that both parties share. Present a revised plan with the best and most feasible ideas from each group, allowing all to enjoy some ownership of the final plan.

- **Keep the number of persons you involve in the solution to a minimum.** Focus on the thoughts of the individuals you know will be most affected.

Maximize Volunteer Motivation

Many local affiliates of Americus, GA-based Habitat for Humanity International (HFH) operate their own ReStore, an open-to-the-public retail outlet that sells donated building materials, fixtures and furnishings at a reduced cost.

For the Greater Albuquerque chapter of HFH (Albuquerque, NM), it took one passionate volunteer, Ruth Friesen, to bring its ReStore into being. Today, the Albuquerque ReStore is so financially successful, it covers the Greater Albuquerque HFH's entire operating expenses.

Friesen shares tips to make the most of your volunteer workforce:

- If a volunteer wants to create a project — and has the passion to prove it can be done, along with the willingness to make it happen — say yes. "I volunteered for a year prior to opening the store, wrote a business plan, visited several other ReStores and scouted potential buildings," says Friesen, adding that she had not been specifically asked to, but did so on her own initiative.

- Suggest sponsorships, scholarships and contests from which volunteers can draw further motivation. Friesen won a local Chamber of Commerce contest for the best business plan; part of the prize was publicity for ReStore through a local radio station.

- Do not fear your volunteers! Friesen says her greatest frustration during her yearlong project was encountering trepidation by the board of directors whose members feared that they would sink money into a project that would fail, even though the concept had proved successful in other cities.

- When the time comes, say yes. "The board kept telling me to continue investigating for the entire year, until finally I told them if they couldn't commit, I had better things to do with my time," says Friesen. "At that point they realized they had a ready and eager volunteer they were about to lose, and that spurred the go-ahead." Remember, Friesen says, that an enthusiastic volunteer is one of your organization's most valuable resources.

Source: Ruth Friesen, Founder, ReStore, Albuquerque, NM. Phone (506) 217-0130. E-mail: rpfriesen@comcast.net. Website: www.habitatabq.org

Make Time to Walk the Walk

Do you have volunteers who regularly perform tasks efficiently with little or no staff involvement? If so, work by their side for a shift or two.

By walking in their shoes, you will better understand their work experience and discover ways to make their work more rewarding for them. Be observant of things such as:

- **Work environment** — proper lighting, noise level, adequate space, comfort and other physical aspects that may need to be changed.

- **Work process** — who does what when, steps that may be unnecessary, ideas that may make their work operate more efficiently and effectively and more.

- **Work mood** — camaraderie, personality conflicts, competition and job satisfaction.

Taking time to be part of the volunteers' work experience will help you see tasks from volunteers' perspectives while also sending them the message that you appreciate their efforts and are willing to walk alongside of them to get the job done.

Reduce Compassion Fatigue While Strengthening Resilience

If your organization's mission puts your volunteers, your staff, and even yourself into highly stressful situations, be on the lookout for signs of compassion fatigue.

Compassion fatigue is the extreme state experienced by those helping others in distress and preoccupation with the suffering of those they are helping to the point of traumatizing the volunteer or helper. It can be a common ailment among volunteers who work with clients dealing with traumatic events, health issues or animal welfare.

Kim Heinrichs, executive director of volunteer resources at San Diego Hospice and The Institute for Palliative Medicine (San Diego, CA), shares signs her organization uses to determine if someone is experiencing compassion fatigue:

- Inability to define healthy boundaries.

- Desire or need to fix patients' problems.

- Hesitation to share volunteer intervention with staff team members.

- Believing that patient can't survive without his/her help.

- Feeling of hopelessness as though nothing he/she does will make anything better.

Heinrichs shares steps to go from compassion fatigue to professional resilience:

- Take a break between patient or client assignments.
- Participate in supportive supervision meetings and

continuing education and accept support from volunteer staff or the coordinator.

- Discover and commit to personal self-care, including exercise, gardening, meditation or other forms of relaxation.

- Open communication between volunteer and staff to tackle potential patient or family challenges before they become a problem.

"Managers must understand that burnout is real and exists for both volunteers and staff," Heinrichs says. "Commit to best training and support practices by using training modules, available from national organizations such as the National Hospice and Palliative Care Organization (Alexandria, VA) and Volunteering in America (Washington, D.C.)." She recommends training modules that incorporate key topics such as saying goodbye, compassionate listening, boundary issues and best practices to educate and support volunteers.

Finally, Heinrichs says, be approachable and understanding, so volunteers will seek help from the management team. Enforce clear, ongoing communication between volunteer coordinators by instituting check-in calls to facilitate safe, open dialogue.

Source: Kim Heinrichs, Executive Director of Volunteer Resources, San Diego Hospice and The Institute for Palliative Medicine, San Diego, CA. Phone (619) 278-6458.
E-mail: KHeinrichs@SDHospice.org. Website: www.sdhospice.org

Three Ways to Ensure Success of Your Volunteer Committees

When it comes to successful volunteer committees, "Everyone needs to check their egos at the door," says Elaine Honig, founder and president, Wine, Women & Shoes (Sonoma, CA).

Honig knows about working successfully with volunteer teams. Her company has provided licensing and consultation for Wine, Women & Shoes events in 25 cities, with more than 15,000 attendees and more than $4.5 million raised for their charity partners to date.

Each of these events is run locally by a volunteer committee.

Here, Honig shares three key factors all volunteer managers can put into play to create effective volunteer teams:

1. Be realistic. Know who is on your committee and what their strengths are, being unflinchingly honest about what each person brings to the table. Make every attempt to use volunteers in capacities for which they are best suited.

2. Break tasks down into small, pure bites. "The PR person should really just be handling PR," says Honig. This means volunteers shouldn't be assigned extra tasks just because there is no one else to do them. Keeping volunteers focused on their piece of the pie helps the whole event run more smoothly.

3. Get the right chairperson. That person should be playful, supportive and fun. Honig says she has seen overwhelmed committee chairs shoot down volunteers who come to them with great ideas. "They can say no a lot, which is disempowering to committee members. This can make members just want to get through an event and then never do it again," which is not good for the long-term success of your organization.

Source: Elaine Honig, Founder and President, Wine, Women & Shoes, 2400 Grove St., Sonoma, CA 94574. Phone (707) 479-2055. E-mail: elaine@winewomenandshoes.com.

Techniques to Set Your Drifting Volunteers Back on Course

Finding talented people and persuading them to volunteer for your cause is a major challenge on its own. Keeping volunteers happy and productive is an even loftier goal.

Being sensitive to each individual's level of satisfaction can help in those efforts if you recognize some of the signals drifting volunteers project. Once you notice these types of signals, try one or more of these strategies to keep volunteers interested and active:

- Be sure they have assignments that suit their skills and talents. A people-oriented person may not complain about a job that requires little interaction with others, but may feel his/her true abilities are not being recognized.

- Are they paired with a more aggressive person who appears to run the show? If you are aware that a quiet person has been working closely with a more flamboyant type, make a special effort to point out the accomplishments of the silent partner as well.

- Spend one-on-one time with those you feel drifting away. Invite them for coffee and ask for their ideas. This positive connection can lead to more successful interaction.

- Look for signs of personality conflicts with others on the team. The solution may be as simple as offering each assignments where little collaboration is needed.

- Are personal matters keeping their minds off of work? Even if they won't share details, let them know that everyone has times when they must focus on family or career matters.

- Evaluate if you are able to offer ongoing opportunities the volunteer seeks. Some people may be better suited as independent contractors with your organization. You may have an ideal one-time job for them. Encourage them to continue as contributing members with a flexible schedule.

- Visit with them about their goals and hopes for your organization. You may discover that their ideas and your mission simply aren't a good fit. If so, brainstorm to discover a particular duty that makes the volunteer feel he/she is helping to take your organization in a mutually rewarding direction.

- Have you done your part to make meetings efficient and convenient for the drifter? Their work style may be nose to the grindstone, while yours is more relaxed and social, yet still productive.

- Do they feel appreciated and valued? Some volunteers prefer to work quietly and without too many words of thanks that draw attention to them. Others thrive on constant reinforcement and recognition. Find the proper balance for satisfying the potential drifter's needs without giving an impression of favoritism.

- Ask their friends for insight. You won't look like you're pressing for confidential information with a few discreet inquiries. A simple observation such as, "Liz did such a fine job on that event last year, what might be an equally interesting task for her this fall?" will begin a flow of information from those who know her outside of the organization.

- Let them know you view them as having a bright future with your organization, and that you have satisfying projects coming. They may be under the impression that they have done all they can, not realizing new challenges exist.

Eight Steps to Resolving Conflicts With Volunteers

Managing volunteers is not unlike managing paid employees, identifying problems and developing a path for improvement can only lead to the strengthening of your volunteer organization.

If you've been experiencing problems with a volunteer such as tardiness or some other human resources-related issue, consider having a meeting one-on-one with the volunteer. Use this face-to-face, confidential discussion to address the issue and set forth a plan for correction.

In the process, follow these easy steps to conflict resolution:

- *Step 1:* Schedule a time to have the meeting at a private location. Provide the volunteer ample notice to attend.
- *Step 2:* The day of the meeting, review the intentions and expectations for the outcome of the meeting.
- *Step 3:* Clearly state the issue at hand and thoroughly describe the expectations of volunteers specific to the issue at your nonprofit.

- *Step 4:* Allow the volunteer to explain his/her position without interrupting. Once the volunteer has expressed his/her side of the issue, reflect that information back to the volunteer to ensure you understood the explanation.
- *Step 5:* Together, develop at least three courses of action to improve the issue at hand. Offer the volunteer two of the options as a plan of action.
- *Step 6:* Write down the corrective course of action and ask the volunteer to review it for clarity and agreement. Ask them to sign the course of action to emphasize the importance of corrective behavior.
- *Step 7:* Summarize the discussions and have the volunteer repeat in his/her own words what was decided for improvement.
- *Step 8:* Set a time to meet within two weeks to review the issue and ensure that it has been addressed to the satisfaction of you and your volunteer.

Stay Tuned In to Identify Volunteers' Life Cycles

One of the primary reasons volunteers agree to assist an organization is because they enjoy contributing their skills and knowledge for a worthwhile cause. But they also have a variety of reasons for choosing your particular institution, such as working with their friends, having more opportunities to be assigned to jobs they love to do, and identifying strongly with your mission and purpose.

When the combination of these reasons are well balanced, volunteers may spend many years generously offering time and talents to your cause. But if these reasons change and they no longer feel a solid bond with the organization, their enthusiasm will likely weaken as well.

Because both your organization and individual volunteers are constantly active and evolving, changing or expanding in scope, a natural cycle of involvement typically exists between most organizations and their volunteers. And even if the volunteer naturally becomes less active, he/she will be able to pass the baton to a newer volunteer waiting for a chance to do the same with a different approach.

Realizing that the natural life cycle of volunteering varies greatly from person to person, consider these approaches to keeping the flow moving in an orderly direction, which will help ensure more seamless transitions as changes inevitably occur within the structure of your volunteer team:

- **Determine the length of service for key positions.** When you have an unusually talented group of volunteers together, ask if they would commit to a term of two to three years and train a replacement group during their last year. Your new group will have a strong background for their duties, and have time to see others in action that may be qualified to replace them.

- **Communicate with volunteers who are especially valuable.** All volunteers are appreciated and highly valued, yet some stand out as gifted and innovative. They may have more than one skill to share, but still have difficulty finding a niche with your organization. Work as closely with them as possible, even offering a five-year plan with the combination of variety and consistency they seek as a volunteer.

- **Establish both long- and short-term responsibilities.** Some volunteer duties, such as chairmanships of major events, fall neatly into a one-time category. A past chairman can then become an advisory chairman or honorary chairman. But other assignments benefit from consistency and prior experience. Ask volunteers how they feel about doing the same job more than one year — they may be eager to serve a second time after having learned the ropes, or they will know the job is not right for them.

- **Find a place for both one-time and lifetime volunteers.** Depending on their individual personalities and skills, some volunteers will be straightforward about how long they intend to be involved with your organization. They may have career or family plans that affect their length of service, hope to make contacts in as many organizations as possible, or want to offer the same skill to more organizations rather than doing many jobs for just one. Graciously accept volunteer help on the volunteer's terms. One person offering expert assistance on a one-time basis when it is most needed can be as beneficial as years of service by a marginally enthusiastic lifetime member. Both types are valuable, but for different reasons.

Useful Policies, Examples and Forms for the Volunteer Manager

TRACKING VOLUNTEERS' INVOLVEMENT AND IMPACT

How do you justify the time and expense put into your volunteer program? How do you know what effect volunteers are having on your organization's programs and services? How do you know what volunteers are even doing from day to day? Being able to measuring volunteers' activities and impact is crucial to the long term health of your volunteer program, and the following articles offer tools and resources to do just that.

Strong Benefits of Tracking Volunteer Hours

Residents of the Fargo, ND area are encouraged to volunteer their time and track their service through the GiveBack Initiative inspired by the Impact Foundation (Fargo, ND).

The GiveBack with Impact site at www.impactgiveback. org connects persons who wish to donate their hours, talent and service with nonprofits of their choosing to create a positive impact in North Dakota and the western Minnesota communities. The site features a searchable database of volunteer opportunities, a portal for compiling volunteer service data and an outlet for the philanthropic to donate to member nonprofits. Volunteers track their hours and monetary donations through an online confidential account.

Jim Manly, Impact Foundation's director of volunteer initiatives, says the online volunteer tracking system:

✓ Allows volunteers and nonprofits to track time spent volunteering, which can be translated into donated funds by multiplying hours served by the current national volunteer rate.

✓ Lets volunteers and nonprofits review contributed time and donations.

✓ Provides data to help volunteers qualify for the President's Volunteer Service Award from the Points of Light Foundation (Washington, D.C.) and other honors. "When hours are tracked," Manly says, "other possibilities for reward and recognition can easily be offered."

Source: Jim Manly, Director of Volunteer Initiatives, Impact Foundation, Fargo, ND. Phone (877) 977-5770. E-mail: jimmanly@impactfdn.org. Website: www.impactgiveback.org

Helper List Organizes Duties

With the help of 50 to 100 volunteers every month, the Marin County Bicycle Coalition (MCBC) of Fairfax, CA, improves county roads and bike path facilities for walkers and bikers in Marin County.

Coalition members and volunteers go to the volunteer page at the MCBC website (www.marinbike.org) to see the organization's growing list of helpers. They can find breakdowns by quarter of who's been helping in the following departments: office/technical support, news distribution, outreach, fundraising, legal advice, advocacy, bike parking, Share the Road, Safe Routes to School, Teens Go Green and the Bikers Ball.

Jo Ann Richards, volunteer and activities coordinator, lists three primary reasons for naming volunteer helpers by department:

• Doing so provides specific acknowledgement of how the volunteers are helping.

• It shows how many volunteers are needed for the different aspects of the organization.

• Acknowledgement by way of a fiscal year list of helpers also inspires others to pitch in and help the organization.

Source: Jo Ann Richards, Volunteer & Activities Coordinator, Marin County Bicycle Coalition, Fairfax, CA. Phone (415) 456-3469. E-mail: joann@marinbike.org. Website: www.marinbike.org

Do Unexpected Spot Checks Make Sense for You?

Do you ever peek in on volunteers while they're working to evaluate their work as it is being performed? Regular but unexpected spot checks represent one of several ways to evaluate volunteer performance.

While this evaluative method may not work for some volunteer tasks, it can prove useful in a number of instances — observing volunteer receptionists, tour guides, speakers,

those who work with those you serve, and more.

To better manage a procedure for conducting regular spot checks, develop a report of your own using the example provided below. Such a report serves as both a reminder (to conduct spot checks regularly) and a record (to collectively show the results of spot checks). The reports can then be referred to when doing semiannual or yearly performance evaluations.

Volunteer Spot-check Evaluations

Evaluator _____

Date	Time	Volunteer	Title/Duty	Comments

Online Form Allows Volunteers to Independently Track Hours

Consider offering an online volunteer-service-hours form to assist your volunteer office in compiling data.

At the University of Rhode Island (Kingston, RI), students can find resources and assistance for volunteer opportunities at its Feinstein Center for Service Learning. But this main volunteer office does not capture all volunteering done by the 16,000 students. So to capture as much of the campus volunteer activity as possible, Sarah Miller, volunteer coordinator, recently launched an online tool.

The form, found at www.uri.edu/volunteer/servicehrs, allows students to log service hours to better track volunteer efforts among the campus community.

"This is a very service-focused campus, our students are so engaged in the community," says Sarah Miller, volunteer coordinator. "The students don't always contact the volunteer office because (volunteering) is something they just do naturally. Because of this, I implemented the online log form to start tracking all the service done on campus, even efforts not coordinated at the Feinstein Center, so we have a better understanding of the impact of our students in the community."

The form captures this data:

❑ Student organization
❑ Name and title
❑ E-mail address
❑ Date of service
❑ Number of hours completed
❑ Number of volunteer participants
❑ Number of faculty/staff participants
❑ Project/organization identification
❑ Brief description of volunteer effort

Currently the information goes directly to the university's volunteer office, where staff collect it manually. As the form becomes more commonplace and readily used by students on a regular basis, Miller intends to connect the form to a database that will compile volunteer data for evaluation. Student service interns will connect with student clubs to spread the word about utilizing the form within the volunteer-oriented student body.

Source: Sarah Miller, Volunteer Coordinator, The University of Rhode Island, Kingston, RI. Phone (401) 874-7422. E-mail: sgmiller@mail.uri.edu. Website: www.uri.edu/volunteer

Timeline Helpful in Managing Multiple Projects

Managing multiple volunteer-driven projects requires a juggler's finesse. To truly manage volunteers who in turn manage and carry out various projects requires the ability to keep one eye on the big picture while, at the same time, providing ongoing support for those involved with carrying out each step of each project or program.

To help you monitor and manage several projects/programs simultaneously, the use of a multiple project/program timeline is critical. Whatever form such a timeline takes, it should provide you with a snapshot of all current projects as well as key actions scheduled to take place within each project.

The timeline example, at right, is intended to illustrate how you can develop one suitable to your own needs and circumstances.

MULTIPLE PROJECT/PROGRAM TIMELINE — As of: _____

Project/Program	Date	Action	Responsible	Comments
Community Service	8/10	Enlist chairperson	McCarthy	
Project	9/10	Enlist executive committee	Chairperson	
	10/10	Recruit additional volunteers	Executive committee	
	11/10	Secure one or more sponsors	Executive committee	
	12/10	Publicize project community-wide	Executive committee	
	1//11	Carry out community project	Exec. committee/others	
	1//11	Cleanup/follow-up	Exec. committee/others	
Orientation Workshop	7/10	Enlist co-chairs	McCarthy	
	8/10	Plan/review procedures	McCarthy/co-chairs	
	8/10	Orientation letters sent	Staff	
	9/10	Orientation workshop	McCarthy/co-chairs	
Adopt a Business	9/10	Enlist co-chairs	McCarthy	
	10/10	Enlist committee members	Co-chairs	
	11/10	Review/assign business calls	Committee members	
	1/11	Calls completed	Committee members	
	2/11	Follow-up completed	Committee members	
Letter-writing	10/10	Enlist chairperson	McCarthy	
Campaign	11/10	Enlist committee members	Chairperson	
	12/10	Letter-writing day	Committee members	
Chili Cookoff	11/10	Enlist co-chairs	McCarthy	
Fundraiser	1/11	Recruit planning committee	Co-chairs	
	2/11	Recruit additional volunteers	Planning committee	
	3/11	Marketing/publicity	Planning committee	
	3/11	Chili Cookoff	Planning committee/others	

Online Account Sign-up Eases Volunteer Management

Metro Volunteers (Denver, CO) is an organization dedicated to helping individuals, volunteers, corporate and community groups find volunteer opportunities. This nonprofit has helped engage more than 200,000 volunteers since 1994.

To effectively manage the organization's active volunteers, Metro Volunteers staff has developed an online volunteer account sign-up system to track the activity of more than 7,000 enrolled volunteers. Volunteers simply visit www.metrovolunteers.com and complete the online sign-up page to enroll.

"The volunteer account is much like a resume so that volunteers can better manage their volunteer careers," says Kristen York, marketing and communications.

Through the online enrollment form, volunteers enter their contact information, e-mail address and phone number, availability and areas of interest and skill set; determine if they would like to enroll for the e-newsletter; and share how they learned of the organization.

As volunteer opportunities arise, staff evaluate enrolled volunteers based on their skill level and availability to determine whether to notify them of openings. The volunteer accounts also assist volunteer managers with training and tracking volunteer hours. Project leaders also benefit from the volunteer account system as they can easily coordinate efforts with participating volunteers in their project.

The volunteer account also helps track what volunteers give back to the community. After a project wraps, volunteers are encouraged to take the time to log in to fill in the details of the finished project.

Source: Kristen York, Marketing and Communications, Metro Volunteers, Denver, CO. Phone (303) 282-1234.
E-mail: YorkK@MetroVolunteers.org.
Website: www.metrovolunteers.org

Completion Card Lets You Know Who's Done What, When

Find it challenging to get volunteers to complete assigned projects on time? A simple project completion card might add that extra push that some volunteers need.

When you make specific volunteer assignments, include a project completion card like the one shown here. Include the assignment and deadline date on the card and instruct the volunteer to return the self-mailer to you — have your name and address preprinted on the back of the card — as soon as the project has been completed.

Ask the volunteer to include the date of completion along with pertinent comments.

Not only does the card add a degree of accountability for the volunteer, not receiving it alerts you to assignments that may not be completed by the deadline.

WEIGLAND ART CENTER
MEMBERSHIP CAMPAIGN

Please return this self-mailing card
as soon as your calls have been completed. Thank you.

Name Marianne Walsh

Assigned Project
Make membership calls on — 1. Robert and Mary Haeger
2. Adelle Peterson 3. Mark Watson

Project Deadline 8/25 **Date Completed** 8/20

Results/Comments *Haegers gave $100; Adelle bought a family membership and Mark is checking with his boss about a company membership.*

Plan Acknowledges Contributed Hours

To encourage and motivate volunteers to strive for more hours, create a yearlong recognition system based on contributed hours. Prepare a chart, such as the illustration here, that volunteers will readily see when they report to work.

Set mile-marker hour goals for the year. Then when a volunteer hits a milestone, date the chart for that person and give him/her a memento of the occasion: a lapel pin, inclusion in a 500-hours club with certain perks, etc. You may even choose to make the award in the presence of all your volunteers.

The Road to Achievement Contributed Hours Recognition for 2011							
	Mile-marker Hours						
Volunteer	10	25	50	100	250	500	1,000

Weekly Volunteer Surveys Gather Valuable Information

Conducting weekly volunteer surveys informs and enlightens staff concerning areas needing improvement at Free Arts Minnesota (Minneapolis, MN).

With the assistance of 150 weekly mentor volunteers, this nonprofit introduces the healing powers of artistic expression to abused, neglected and at-risk children and their families. Through its weekly mentorship program, four to six volunteers form a team that leads weekly small group art sessions with children September through May. Small group sessions include visual arts, dance, drama, music, creative writing and more.

To keep a handle on its vast volunteer program, Esther Callahan, volunteer coordinator, asks mentor teams to complete weekly surveys available at the www. freeartsminnesota.org website. Information gleaned from surveys helps this nonprofit in many ways including volunteer involvement, program evaluation and constituent satisfaction.

Callahan shares specific ways the surveys help improve day-to-day volunteer operations:

- The completed surveys help identify the dynamics of the population served and provide that information for grant proposals.

- Weekly updates aid in defining constituent needs and results as well as allowing for information sharing with donors.

- Surveys gather project curriculum information and allow Free Arts Minnesota to share this information with mentors in the monthly newsletter.

- Information obtained via weekly surveys helps the volunteer coordinator determine that volunteers are on the job and active each week.

- Completion of regular surveys helps Free Arts Minnesota to evaluate the number of constituents served and evaluate any dramatic changes in constituent need.

Source: Esther Callahan, Volunteer Coordinator, Free Arts Minnesota, Minneapolis, MN. Phone (612) 824-2787. E-mail: Esther@freeartsminnesota.org. Website: www.freeartsminnesota.org

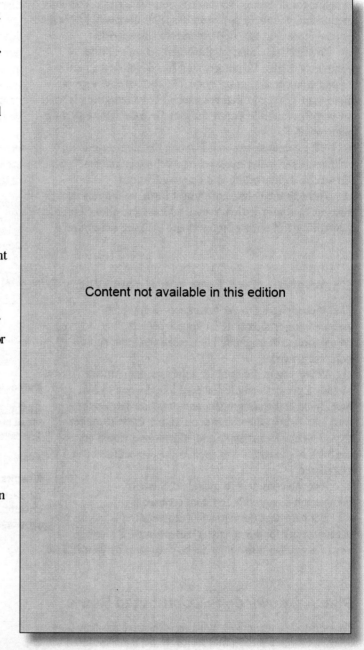

Content not available in this edition

Useful Policies, Examples and Forms for the Volunteer Manager.
Edited by Scott C. Stevenson.
© 2011 Stevenson, Inc. Published 2011 by Stevenson, Inc.

Useful Policies, Examples and Forms for the Volunteer Manager

IDEAS FOR THANKING AND RECOGNIZING VOLUNTEERS

In many ways, recognition is the closest thing to a paycheck volunteers receive. People volunteer for a variety of reasons, but sincere appreciation is almost always a key ingredient in motivating them to return year after year. The following articles offer a range of new and unique ideas for your recognition and appreciation initiatives.

Recognize Volunteers Every Step of the Way

At the Seattle Aquarium (Seattle, WA), volunteers are not only recognized for years of service, but hours of service.

Each and every milestone of service is rewarded with a variety of perks and the listing of the volunteer's name in the organization's newsletter, the All Wet Gazette.

"Some volunteers are with us for years, but can only give a few hours, while others can give a lot of hours but may not serve more than five or 10 years — we recognize both hours and years served," says Sue Donohue Smith, guest experience manager.

"By recognizing volunteers at the small levels, you set them up to stay with you."

At the aquarium, volunteers serving 100, 250, 500, 1,000 and every 1,000 hours after receive a certificate in appreciation of their efforts and recognition in the newsletter.

In addition, volunteers who have reached their first 100 hours of service receive a patch for their uniform. They then receive rockers, which are smaller patches that fit around the large patch that signify different jobs, every five years of service and every 1,000 hours of service. Also, all volunteers receive pins for every year of service, with each pin portraying a different animal.

All volunteers receive the monthly newsletter and Weekly Critter News publications as a perk, as well as invitations to socials and picnics including the Dive Social and Exotic Team picnic.

Volunteers are also invited to staff meetings to instill their importance to the organization, and receive one entrance ticket for every 25 hours served, plus a free family membership after six months of service.

"By recognizing volunteers at the small levels, you set them up to stay with you," says Donohue Smith. "The bottom line is that volunteers at the Seattle Aquarium know they are important and critical to our success. They learn this on day one, and it is reinforced to them constantly."

Follow the lead of the Seattle Aquarium, recognize your volunteers at every milestone no matter how big or small.

Source: Sue Donohue Smith, Guest Experience Manager, Seattle Aquarium, Seattle, WA. Phone (206) 399-7033.
E-mail: sue.donohue-smith@seattle.gov

Recognize and Celebrate Your Volunteers Every Day

Volunteer recognition traditionally occurs at an annual event. But don't ignore opportunities the other 364 days of the year. Here are a few suggestions to honor volunteers:

- Put up a bulletin board in your lobby or front office. Fill it with photos of volunteers in action and letters from constituents affected by their service.
- Invite the volunteers to a staff meeting.
- When they arrive for their shift, greet individuals by name and thank them for coming. When they leave, ask how their shift went and thank them again.
- If your volunteers use a touch-screen computer to check in and out, send customized greetings to thank and recognize the volunteers for their accomplishments.
- Schedule time in your day to meet with your volunteers.
- Greet them with a smile, handshake, hug or a pat on the back.
- Surprise the volunteers with fun treats and surprises (e.g., snacks, lottery tickets, ice cream, freebies).
- Compliment the volunteer in public.
- Write thank-you notes.

- Make regular phone calls to just say hi.
- Visit various work sites to interact with the volunteers.
- Show an interest in their health, hobbies and family.
- Encourage staff to call to say how much they appreciate the volunteers' service.
- Feature volunteers on your organization's website with a picture and a story on what they do to make a difference in the community.
- Make it a point to remember every volunteer's name and use it when interacting.
- Send a note or card to celebrate a special event (e.g., birthday, anniversary) or let them know you are thinking of them at a difficult time (e.g., if they or a loved one are in the hospital, death in the family). Encourage your CEO to send a note as well.
- Buy them lunch.

Whether doing so means putting reminders in your planner or placing self-stick notes on your computer monitor, constantly remind yourself to make daily recognition a habit rather than something that is easily overlooked.

Honor Volunteers by Donating in Their Names

Consider offering a monetary award to add a philanthropic touch to your next volunteer awards ceremony.

Whatcom Volunteer Center (Bellingham, WA) has celebrated volunteers in Whatcom County through its Heart & Hands Award since 2000. The center works to match volunteers with 350 nonprofits, schools, government agencies and healthcare organizations serving the region.

To earn the Heart & Hands Award presented at the Celebration of Service event each April, volunteers are nominated by colleagues, fellow volunteers and community members.

In 2010, the center received 54 nominations and, of those, three jurors selected five volunteers as final candidates. All five honorees received a certificate of appreciation, engraved vase and recognition in front of 250 guests at the volunteer appreciation event. Recipients also received written acknowledgement at the center's website detailing their outstanding service.

Each volunteer also received a special philanthropic gift, says Sue Ellen Heflin, executive director. "The selected award winners received a donation made in their name to the nonprofit of their choice," says Heflin. "This year, five awards of $200 each were given to nonprofits of the award recipient's choosing."

Source: Sue Ellen Heflin, Executive Director, Whatcom Volunteer Center, Bellingham, WA. Phone (360) 734-3055.
E-mail: SueEllenH@whatcomvolunteer.org. Website: www.whatcomvolunteer.org

Content not available in this edition

List Volunteers' Collective Contributions

While it's great to use your newsletter to publicly thank volunteers, including a regular section that summarizes collective volunteer contributions goes even further to:

1. **Instill group pride.** The list really helps all volunteers — and everyone else on your mailing list — visualize what they have accomplished in recent weeks or months.

2. **Show the big picture.** When volunteers are assisting with a particular project, such a listing helps them see all of the additional accomplishments being made.

3. **Help paid staff evaluate use of volunteer time.** Listing collective volunteer accomplishments periodically forces paid staff to better evaluate how volunteers are being utilized.

4. **Justify the volunteer budget for the boss.** The regular list of collective accomplishments is a meaningful way to let upper management and your board see the positive impact volunteers have on programs and services.

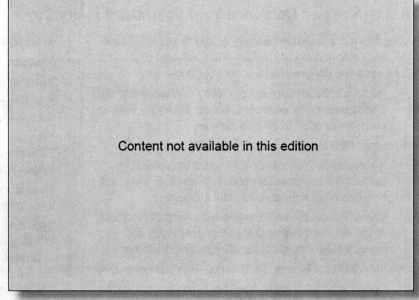

Content not available in this edition

IDEAS FOR THANKING AND RECOGNIZING VOLUNTEERS

Recognize Top Mentors

Mentors comprise a large part of the volunteer program at the Community Partnership for Children (Daytona Beach, FL). Each year, the organization — dedicated to child protection through services, mentoring and advocating for children in need — recognizes a local volunteer with the Distinguished Friend of Children award.

"We believe it is important to recognize our mentors, because they are such a valuable part of helping to heal a child," says Jo Lynn Deal, chief communications officer. "Mentors are terrific advocates for children and the program and by them sharing their positive experiences, we're able to recruit many new mentors to the program.'

The organization currently has 14 mentors matched with children and nine in the screening process awaiting a match.

The award program helps draw welcome attention to the program, she says.

" Recognizing top performers can serve as a wonderful recruitment tool for new mentors and a training opportunity for existing mentors. By nature, our mentors are people who want to help, and this also includes helping each other to be successful mentors."

The organization also recognizes mentors in its newsletter, on its website, through news coverage and media outreach, plus through weekly correspondence and encouraging feedback. Twice each year a mentor dinner is held to bring all mentors together to network and celebrate their accomplishments.

Source: Susan Hiltz, Mentor Service Coordinator, and Jo Lynn Deal, Chief Communications Officer, Community Partnership for Children, Daytona Beach, FL. Phone (386) 547-2293. E-mail: Jolynn.Deal@cbcvf.org. Website: www.communitypartnershipforchildren.org

Four Easy Holiday Volunteer Recognition Ideas

Try these simple, effective ways to honor the work your volunteers do this season:

1. **Ask board members to write letters or cards to volunteers.** Divide the list of volunteer names among the board along with bullet points of ways the volunteer serves your nonprofit to assist the board member in writing a meaningful message.

2. **Create a catered affair with staff bringing dishes for a potluck honoring volunteers.** Enjoy the meal together and ask participants to raise a glass to volunteers' efforts. Encourage sharing of positive, volunteer-related memories from the year.

3. **Host a secret gift exchange.** Set a price range, then recruit willing staff or board members, matching each with one volunteer and directions to provide secret accolades and small gifts. Offer volunteer-specific suggestions, such as a gas gift card for the volunteer who drives 30 miles one-way to help your cause, or a basket of gift tags and bags for the volunteer expecting a household of grandchildren for the holidays.

4. **Conduct a gratitude roundtable.** This could be a simple gathering of volunteers, volunteer managers, select clients and staff to discuss the year's accomplishments, recognize major volunteer achievements and develop efforts for the coming year.

Offer Your Volunteers Symbols of Gratitude

Make your volunteers feel special with these symbols of your appreciation:

❑ **Group photo:** Frame a group photo of all current volunteers with the front row holding a poster, complete with the organization's logo, displaying the year. Take this photo each year at the same time and distribute to your current volunteer base. Don't forget to display a large copy of the photo in your lobby or reception area.

❑ **Another group photo:** Organize a group photo of willing clients of your organization holding a large thank-you poster. Give a copy to each volunteer. This added

touch will mean a lot to your steadfast volunteers.

❑ **Thank-you card:** Each year, have all staff and management sign thank-you cards for each volunteer (or volunteer group/team). Request that each person add a personal, heartfelt note specific to that volunteer/volunteer group.

❑ **Invitation:** Invite individual volunteers to join in on a coffee break or casual continental breakfast with the head of the organization. If possible, create small-group opportunities for volunteers to attend a coffee with the head of the organization monthly or quarterly on a rotating basis.

RSVPs Ensure Seamless Volunteer Recognition Event

Knowing how many volunteers and guests to expect at your volunteer recognition event can allow you to properly plan this important celebration.

A registration form doubled as an RSVP form for the volunteer recognition event for the Arthritis Foundation Eastern Pennsylvania Chapter (Pennsylvania, PA), helping organizers know how many attendees and attendees' guests to expect at the March 2010 breakfast buffet/awards ceremony.

Of the nearly 1,300 volunteers invited, more than 210 returned RSVPs.

"We want our recognition events to have a fun and energetic feel to match the personalities of our spectacular volunteers," says Wade Balmer, director of operations and mission integration. "This is an event to pump volunteers up, honor them and show them how much we appreciate their volunteerism. The event isn't long — it's on a Saturday from 10 a.m. to 12 noon. (The Pennsylvania suburb of) King of Prussia is chosen as the location because it's easy to find, accessible via public transportation and several major roads and people can make a day of it and shop at the mall afterwards."

Balmer says that because each volunteer is presented with a certificate of appreciation at the recognition event, asking volunteers to RSVP assisted planners in preparing certificates in advance. RSVPs also afforded event planners the opportunity to gauge attendance and prepare the appropriate amount of food for the group.

Balmer adds that the written RSVP registrations have generated interest from persons beyond the organization's volunteer base, allowing the organization to reach out to these people to offer them opportunities to volunteer and/or give to the cause.

Source: Wade Balmer, Director of Operations and Mission Integration, Arthritis Foundation-Eastern Pennsylvania Chapter, Philadelphia, PA. Phone (215) 971-5476. E-mail: wbalmer@arthritis.org. Website: www.arthritis.org

This RSVP form, included in the event flyer and online, helped organizers of a volunteer recognition event for the Arthritis Foundation-Eastern Pennsylvania Chapter (Philadelphia, PA) better plan by informing them who would be attending, and if they would bring guests.

Useful Policies, Examples and Forms for the Volunteer Manager

APPROACHES TO EFFECTIVE COMMUNICATION AND OUTREACH

Effective communication underlies almost all aspects of volunteer management. From recruitment and retention to recognition and training, communication allows leaders to not only instruct and direct volunteers, but to instill them with the vision and mission that lie at the heart of the organization. Use the following resources to make your communications as reliable and effective as possible.

Use All Options Available to Communicate With Volunteers

Volunteers lead full lives and have many demands on their time. Communicating with them effectively will ensure that your volunteer events are well managed and that volunteers receive all necessary information to stay on top of their assignments.

Use the following communications tools to reach your volunteers:

1. **Facebook** — Ask current and incoming volunteers to become fans of your organization's Facebook page so they can receive Facebook posts about upcoming volunteer opportunities at your nonprofit.

2. **Website** — Create an event-specific volunteer page at your organization's website where volunteers can get details about your cause, sign up for specific volunteer tasks and garner information about the event.

3. **E-mail blasts** — Use e-mail as your primary communication tool during event planning. Make messages detailed and specific. E-mail announcements to all volunteers involved in the event, to assign specific roles to each volunteer and to keep them posted about changes.

Don't forget to add the critical information as to when the volunteers should arrive, what attire they should be wearing and any items they will need to bring with them.

4. **Text** — Use text messaging to inform volunteers of updates the day of the event. Be sure to get cell numbers in advance of the event, so they are stored in your cell in case notifications need to be sent out. Ask volunteers to contact you by cell phone the day of the event to avoid any errant messages that you won't get by e-mail or office voicemail.

5. **Event newsletter** — Create an event-specific newsletter as a wrap-up to all events that involved volunteers. Use it to inform your volunteers about the success of the event, to send kudos to your high-achieving volunteers and to offer thanks for their individual efforts. Include photos of the volunteers in action, and on the last page, create a thank-you page. On the thank-you page, list all volunteers who participated in the event. Check this list carefully so no name is misspelled and no volunteer is left out.

Let Volunteers, Supporters Tell Your Organization's Story

Sharing your organization's story with the public is more than a matter of selecting events and writing press releases. Remember that every person who dedicates his or her time to your mission sees your story differently. Use that knowledge as you consider unique ways to tell your story:

✓ **Look for unique messengers.** The most compelling people are not always public speakers. Seek out those who have meaningful relationships with your organization and make a video or write a short story about them.

✓ **Let your supporters tell your story.** Host a 100-words-or-less contest where they can tell why they appreciate your programs and services and provide content you can use in advertisements, in publications or on your website.

✓ **Clearly define your call to action.** While you may have a variety of ways to tell your organization's story, focus on and identify one or more intriguing common threads (such as job training for domestic violence survivors) and turn it into a feature article to submit to local publications to use

at any time.

✓ **Ask volunteers to submit videos.** Many people feel comfortable and candid when they can create their own video in their own environment describing why they became involved with your cause. Provide a time limit and two or three questions for them to answer. Post them on your blogs, social media outlets and website.

✓ **Focus on honesty and realism.** Overselling your mission can defeat your purpose if success stories don't ring true. People recognize that small victories for one of your beneficiaries can lead to life-changing long-term accomplishments. Be proud of being a small but significant step in someone's journey and share it openly.

✓ **Find new audiences for your story.** All of your volunteers, clients and supporters know people who are not familiar with your programs. Seek out some of them to speak to members of their churches, civic clubs or academic groups and invite those who show interest to visit your facility for a tour.

Letters of Appreciation Should Be Specific

Which would you prefer: a form letter saying "Thanks for all you've done for us during the past year," or one that not only says "thanks," but personally details your many accomplishments as well? No brainer, isn't it? The letter listing all you did for the organization would be more personal and memorable.

That's one reason to closely monitor and record what volunteers do throughout the year. At year end, you'll be in a much better position to cite each volunteer's accomplishments and contributions.

Whether you track volunteers' hours and types of service or have someone else do so, whether you record it on index cards or in a computer database, you'll have access to that information when you decide to commend him/her for service to your organization. Doing so will tell them you really do pay attention and appreciate their individual sacrifices.

Tracking a volunteer's activities throughout the year enables you to send a personal message illustrating you notice all they do.

Work Activity Summary
Fiscal Year 2010

Volunteer _Rhonda Evans_ Years of Service _12_

Summary of Involvement/Contributions

- Staffed reception desk (4 hours on average) for 23 days (including Easter, 4th of July).
- Assisted with four mailings — stuffing.
- Assisted in gift shop six times in the year.
- Attended one volunteer in-service session.
- Worked on records jobs for 12 hours.

Dear Rhonda:

I know all you do here at St. Mary's Medical Center is an act of love. It's obvious to me and others associated with our hospital. And while I'm aware that you find great reward in your volunteer work, we here at St. Mary's find great reward in your association with us.

I know that in the past year, for instance, you:

- Staffed the reception desk (4 hours on average) for 23 days, including two holidays!
- Assisted with four mailings — stuffing.
- Assisted in the gift shop six times in the year.
- Attended a volunteer in-service session.
- Worked on records jobs for 12 hours.

And I'm sure you accomplished even more than I've listed here. But I want you to know that we are aware of your dedication and so very grateful for the many ways in which you contribute to St. Mary's.

From all of us,

Thank you!

Spread the News With a Volunteer Calling Tree

Many methods used to keep large numbers of volunteers informed can be both demanding and impersonal. Here's a way to contact volunteers personally with accurate and timely information without spending all day on the phone: Organize a calling tree.

1. **Group your volunteer pool into manageable units** of about 10 (or fewer) people. Type each list of 10, including the volunteer's name, home phone number, cell phone number, and the best time of day the volunteer can be reached.

2. **Appoint a group manager.** One person in each group of 10 is appointed manager. When instructed, this individual makes personal phone calls to others on his/her list to disseminate information or gather a response.

3. **Provide accurate information.** If time permits, put instructions and details in writing. Mail, fax, or e-mail information to the manager or, if time is short, phone him/her. Think ahead and provide answers to the most likely asked questions.

4. **Assign a completion time.** Ask managers to report back to confirm all volunteers were contacted and share any pertinent information from conversations.

A calling tree moves swiftly and adds a personal touch. It allows aides to customize the message, while giving volunteers the opportunity to ask questions or air concerns.

APPROACHES TO EFFECTIVE COMMUNICATION AND OUTREACH

Reach Out to Audiences With Simple Electronic Newsletter

An electronic newsletter, or e-newsletter, could be the best communications tool in your toolbox for raising awareness about your organization while attracting media coverage, volunteers and financial support.

One of the most compelling reasons for considering this online method of connecting with your audiences is that it need not be overcomplicated. A simple, clean masthead with your organization's name, logo and contact information can be followed with whatever information you wish to communicate.

That's the design and method behind the e-newsletter for The Loft Literary Center (Minneapolis, MN). Designed to reach out to volunteers, the e-newsletter quickly informs recipients of volunteer opportunities at upcoming events, says Dara Syrkin, associate communications director/ volunteer coordinator.

The nonprofit center staff use the e-mail marketing service, Constant Contact (www.constantcontact.com), to distribute the electronic newsletter to persons in their volunteer database. Using this venue, Syrkin says, helps them quickly and efficiently engage nearly 200 volunteers to serve audience members and artists at literary events.

"The volunteer e-newsletter is great because I reach 550 people quickly and inexpensively," Syrkin says. "I know how effective it is because of the speed at which people respond. The Loft's volunteers are amazing! And, if by chance I don't have enough help for a certain event, I send out a plea and people always respond."

A volunteer e-newsletter can be a call to fill volunteer spaces, a reminder to committed volunteers or a medium for offering more information to volunteers.

Add details to your volunteer e-newsletter to communicate most effectively, Syrkin advises, and shares tips for accomplishing this:

- Don't be afraid to include some volunteer need-to-know information, such as designated arrival time, what to wear and what to expect. For example, add reminders at the top, bottom or side such as: "Friendly reminder: Your volunteer shift begins one hour before the event start time; dress casually; have fun."

- When filling volunteer slots, succinctly state your request in the subject line of the e-mail similar to The Loft's most recent plea, "Still need two volunteers for Loft upcoming events. Please & thank you."

- Include a link to your event calendar where volunteers or those considering volunteering can go for more information about the event.

- Always, always include the contact person's name,

This electronic newsletter keeps persons informed on volunteering opportunities at The Loft Literary Center (Minneapolis, MN) with brief, specific information and directions on how to sign up or learn more.

Content not available in this edition

e-mail address and phone number. Make it easy for volunteers to enlist.

- As you create your e-newsletter repeat the mantra — "short, sweet, inclusive, clear."

Source: Dara Syrkin, Associate Communications Director/Volunteer Coordinator/Editor, A View from the Loft, The Loft Literary Center, Minneapolis, MN. Phone (612) 215-2575. E-mail: dsyrkin@loft.org. Website: www.loft.org

Produce Newsletters That People Can't Wait to Read

Frankly speaking, far too many nonprofits' newsletters to external audiences — donors, volunteers, board members, current and former customers — don't get read because they are just plain boring. Long articles that go on and on, poor-quality photos and more.

To make your newsletter more readable and inviting:

✓ **Include more bite-sized articles**, 100 words or less, in addition to feature articles.

✓ **Find out what your readers want to know.** Conduct reader surveys. Visit with readers one-on-one to get their honest feedback.

✓ **Use only quality, action photos.** No photo is better than a poor photo. Eliminate head shots or posed shots. Use photos that tell a story.

✓ **Add more variety to your newsletter's content**, something for everyone: issues your organization is tackling, accomplishments, profiles of people and events, calendar of upcoming events, news of new or improved services/programs, recent gifts and stories about those being served by your organization.

✓ **Evaluate your newsletter's design and layout.** If you don't have a graphic designer on staff, enlist the help of an experienced professional who can volunteer to help create a more professional-looking template you can use for future issues.

Analyze Social Media Efforts to Measure Return On Investment

You begin by placing an important announcement on your organization's website. Next, you tweet a link to the announcement asking your Twitter followers to check it out. A few days later, you post a synopsis of the announcement on your blog, including a link to the original Web page. You might even send another tweet announcing the blog post.

And because you integrated Twitter into your LinkedIn and Facebook pages, additional fans, friends and contacts receive the news through those outlets.

Such cross-fertilization makes for good communication strategy while providing a body of concrete metrics to gauge social media efforts' effectiveness, says David Sieg, vice president of strategic marketing, YourMembership.com, Inc. (St. Petersburg, FL).

Sieg says the following areas are particularly suited to measurement:

✓ **Inbound clicks.** The amount of traffic social media communications are driving to your website is an important measure of overall impact, says Sieg. How many users are clicking through to your site from your blog? From your Twitter tweets? From your Facebook page? Measure this information and use it.

✓ **Industry links.** Links are the mark of online relevance, and the number of industry groups and prominent bloggers who link to your website suggests the regard in which your organization (or at least its published content) is held, says Sieg.

✓ **Audience.** Whether friends or fans, subscribers or followers, your loyal audience members are another easily tabulated metric. But Sieg cautions that readership is only a first step, and that user-initiated interaction — filling out a contact page, downloading a contact form, reposting your article — should be the primary goal.

✓ **Search engine optimization.** Your organization's organic page rank (the place it appears on a search engine's page of unpaid search results) is a matter of great importance, says Sieg. Not only does it reflect the number of people viewing your content and linking to your posts, it determines how easily potential members will be able to find your online presence. Never ignore a rising or falling page rank.

✓ **Website analytics.** Google Analytics (www.google.com/analytics), the gold standard of free website analysis, can determine many of the previous metrics including clicks, links and referring sites. Website usage patterns revealed by online analytics — how long users view any particular page, what pages users leave your website from, what percentage of users landing on a contact page actually fill out the form — also give clues about user preferences and behavior.

Finally, Sieg says, do not ignore conventional metrics. "Is your membership growing? Is your revenue increasing? Are your services being utilized? These are areas on which social media should be having an impact and therefore should constitute another form of measurement."

Source: David Sieg, Vice President, Strategic Marketing, YourMembership.com, Inc., St. Petersburg, FL. Phone (727) 827-0046. E-mail: dsieg@yourmembership.com. Website: www.yourmembership.com

APPROACHES TO EFFECTIVE COMMUNICATION AND OUTREACH

Grab Attention With Every Story

To make sure you offer stories people want to read, include these key elements, says Teresa Scalzo, director of publications, Carleton College (Northfield, MN) and award-winning editor of the quarterly magazine, Carleton College Voice:

1. First and foremost, you must have good stories.

2. Second, you need good writers. Treat a good writer like gold, whether he/she is a staff writer or a freelancer.

3. Photography and/or illustration. "Good photography is one of the surest ways to turn skimmers into readers," she says. "A compelling photograph will stop a skimmer in his tracks and get him to pay closer attention to the story."

4. Design. Hire a great designer who understands magazine design.

5. Paper and printing. "Producing magazines is hugely expensive. Don't squander your investment by shirking your responsibility at the very end of the process," says Scalzo. "Choose a printer with a solid reputation (and, ideally, one who has experience printing magazines) and work with your sales rep to choose the best quality paper you can afford."

Source: Teresa Scalzo, Director of Publications and Editor, Carleton College Voice, Carleton College, Northfield, MN. Phone (507) 222-5423. E-mail: tscalzo@carleton.edu

Volunteer Blog Promotes Communication

Create a volunteer blog exclusively available to your volunteer management team and your steadfast volunteers to streamline communication within your nonprofit. Consider these benefits of hosting a volunteer blog at your organization's website:

- Volunteer managers can communicate with all volunteers at one time regarding upcoming events, changes to policy, volunteer openings and much more.

- Volunteers have unlimited access to updates within your nonprofit that directly involve them.

- Volunteer coordinators can post volunteer schedules for easy access.

- Volunteers can post status updates regarding their role in an upcoming event.

- Photos of volunteer activities can be easily uploaded to the site.

- Volunteers can recruit additional volunteers by talking up the blog to friends, family and colleagues.

- Event updates, changes or cancellations can be posted immediately to keep all volunteers informed up to and through the day of the event.

- Volunteer activity feedback, kudos and event success details can be added, bringing extra value to your volunteerism activities.

- And finally, a blog can be an archive of your volunteerism activities. Have volunteer coordinators and volunteers post their how-to for creating a particular event and to provide feedback for future positive changes to the event.

Free Sites To Host Your Blog

Use one of these blog hosting sites to start your free volunteer blog today:

- ✓ www.blogger.com
- ✓ www.wordpress.com
- ✓ www.weebly.com

Useful Policies, Examples and Forms for the Volunteer Manager

YOUTH AND MENTORING TOOLS

Though often overlooked, young people represent an important source of support. Not only can their enthusiasm and energy be put to immediate use, young volunteers and interns often transition into paid positions in time, thereby providing a pool of skilled entry-level workers. The following articles will help you enhance your ability to recruit, oversee and interact with this unique constituency.

Create Youth Advisory Council

Introducing an advisory council that targets young people can be an important step for grooming volunteers and future members within your organization. Since 2005, the Alice Paul Institute (API) of Mount Laurel, NJ, has offered a Girls' Advisory Council (GAC) where students, ages 14-18, design and evaluate leadership and history programs within the nonprofit.

API — an organization dedicated to promoting the life and work of Alice Paul, an American suffragist leader and women's equality advocate — continues Paul's mission by promoting girls' leadership groups within their organization.

"Having members of our constituency as a part of our program evaluation has helped keep our programs and initiatives fresh," says Dana Dabek-Milstein, director of leadership programs. "The girls serve as the public face of our leadership program and are very effective at showing the impact of our programs to donors and supporters."

GAC members attend monthly meetings, develop initiatives, support efforts such as Women's Equality Day, participate in the API Speaker's Bureau and perform other volunteer tasks. Members have gone on to serve as facilitators for other programs in the organization and continue to advocate for Alice Paul and API in college.

Dabek-Milstein offers tips for building a youth program:

✓ Work with local teachers such as those from gifted and talented programs to identify founding members.

✓ Ask founding members or alumni to recruit like-minded members.

✓ Groom founding members to become advocates for your mission and to participate as part of your speakers' bureau to recruit new members and speak on behalf of your organization.

✓ Offer educational-based youth programs geared to your council members to promote a strong sense of knowledge and advocacy.

✓ Keep your group defined and small at the outset. Define what qualities a model member will have and build a base of youth members who fit that mold to found your advisory council.

Source: Dana Dabek-Milstein, Director of Leadership Programs, Alice Paul Institute, Mount Laurel, NJ. Phone (856) 231-1885. E-mail: ddmilstein@alicepaul.org. Website: www.alicepaul.org

Icebreakers Help Teens Warm Up to Volunteering

AquaTeens is a successful teenage volunteer program offered at the Texas State Aquarium (Corpus Christi, TX). Volunteers age 14 to 17 assist at the aquarium while participating in the graduated responsibility, four-year program.

Volunteer roles include shoreline trash cleanup, helping in the gift shop, assisting within the family learning center and sea camp and, by the fourth year of volunteering, working with animal husbandry staff.

Beth Davis, the aquarium's manager of volunteers, has been managing AquaTeens for nearly 10 years. In that time, she has found that using icebreakers to start out teen training is the perfect way to get teens to become interactive with other volunteers who are not within their social network of friends.

Davis suggests trying these icebreakers at your next teen volunteer training session to get the attention of young people and assist them in becoming comfortable with new people:

❑ Separate teens into groups using colors or numbers. Do so to make sure teens are not banding with friends and so newcomers to the group are mixed with veterans. The color- or number-coded groups stay together and work together during training.

❑ Give each group a project to finish such as a small but complicated puzzle. The first group to finish is rewarded with a treat.

❑ Have each teen at the table interview the person to his/her right and then introduce that person to the group. This encourages teens to stand and talk to the group, but not about themselves, while also encouraging them to get to know one another.

❑ After large-group training sessions, separate teens into their designated teams to compete against each other in a trivia contest or treasure hunt based on information they learned in the training.

Source: Beth Davis, Manager of Volunteers, Texas State Aquarium, Corpus Christi, TX. Phone (361) 881-1256. E-mail: bdavis@txstateaq.org. Website: www.texasstateaquarium.org

How to Find Quality Junior Volunteers

How do you determine which applicants make quality junior volunteers?

Mary Rahaim, director of volunteer services, The William W. Backus Hospital (Norwich, CT), says for her organization it's important to find youth still in high school who are willing to learn, be accepting of others, understand the importance of privacy and have a professional attitude.

Rahaim has developed a system to find the most qualified candidates. The following is her process:

1. **Send information packets to local high schools.** Rahaim sends about 30 information packets to local high schools in eastern Connecticut. The packets include program information, applications and Rahaim's business card.

2. **Conduct personal interviews.** Rahaim interviews each applicant with a parent or guardian present. "It's important for the families to know what the expectations are so we're all on the same page regarding orientation, attendance and being professional," says Rahaim. During the interview, she observes the candidate's eye contact, alertness, interest in what she is saying and if the applicant asks questions.

3. **Contact references.** "On the application, I ask for a school reference who is mailed an applicant evaluation form. The form rates the youth's ability to accept direction, express feelings and work independently, and on creativity, dependability and maturity," says Rahaim. "I also ask them to list three adjectives that best describe the applicant. These words are a tell-tale sign of what the applicant is like."

Rahaim says the junior volunteer program is limited to 100 volunteers, which include successful junior volunteers from the previous summer. Once the students are accepted, they must attend an eight-hour classroom orientation including fire safety, policy and procedure, a hospital tour and a bed-making and stretcher/wheelchair training.

Source: Mary Rahaim, Director of Volunteer Services, The William W. Backus Hospital, Norwich, CT. Phone (860) 823-6320. E-mail: mrahaim@wwbh.org

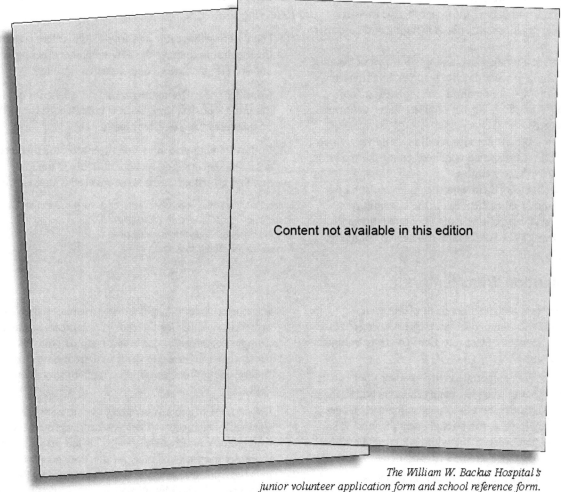

Content not available in this edition

The William W. Backus Hospital's junior volunteer application form and school reference form.

Develop a Skills Profile for Youth Volunteer Positions

A typical volunteer position description explains the purpose and role of the position in the context of the organization, indicates the level of responsibility and outlines the major tasks and responsibilities of the volunteer. However, if your aim is to cultivate learning and skills development, a much more detailed approach is needed.

Start by breaking the position down into its component parts. Analyze each activity to identify what types of skills and knowledge are central (that is, the minimum level of skills needed to perform the tasks). Then, determine which skills a volunteer could develop through training. By listing these two sets of skills, you can create a skills profile for each position or task.

When considering which skills could be developed in a given assignment, you might want to highlight the skills that could be readily transferred to the job market.

Youth Program Leader Skills Profile

- Leadership skills
- Interpersonal skills
- Oral communication skills
- Coaching and mentoring skills
- Teamwork skills
- Teaching and training skills
- Supervising skills
- Planning skills
- Organizational skills
- Creative thinking skills
- Decision-making skills
- Problem-solving skills

Mentor Sessions Guide Volunteers

Having volunteers complete a mentor session can round out training and set volunteers on a long-term path for continued growth at your organization.

At the Atlanta Humane Society (Atlanta, GA), nearly 600 volunteers have undergone special training. Volunteers are educated on the history of the nonprofit, the mission statement of the organization, animal handling and customer service.

In addition to attending two-and-a-half hours of training, volunteers wishing to work directly with pet adoptions and pet-facilitated therapy are required to complete a mentor session to finish their training, says Ashley Vitez, volunteer services manager.

This 150-minute mentor session allows a newly trained volunteer to follow a seasoned volunteer giving them a birds-eye view of their responsibilities.

"The mentor shows them where supplies are and how to do an adoption or takes them out in the community to show them what happens on a pet-facilitated therapy visit," says Vitez. "We have found it has helped volunteer retention, because it can be an intimidating or overwhelming experience coming into a shelter, and this gives them another chance to connect with other volunteers and feel more comfortable."

Vitez recommends the following tips for implementing mentoring sessions at your facility:

❏ Have a knowledgeable and friendly volunteer conduct the mentoring to make the new volunteers feel welcome and solidify the knowledge learned in training.

❏ Consider only offering mentoring on weekends or your nonprofit's busiest time, so new volunteers have plenty of examples from which to learn.

❏ Follow up with your new volunteer after the mentoring session to ensure they feel comfortable in their new role and that all critical items were covered with their mentor.

Source: Ashley Vitez, Volunteer Services Manager, Atlanta Humane Society, Atlanta, GA. Phone (404) 974-2822. E-mail: volunteer@atlantahumane.org. Website: www.atlantahumane.org

Boost Retention With Mentors

Aligning volunteers with mentors from within your organization and the community can create a stronger sense of mission and boost volunteer retention. To create volunteer-mentor relationships:

✓ Ask leaders from corporations that sponsor your events or support your mission to identify mentors within their ranks who can be resources to your volunteers. Does this company have a professional event planner? If so, ask to align that professional with your special events volunteers to create a stronger support network.

✓ Identify leaders within your nonprofit to act as volunteer mentors. Could a board member with specific professional skills lead a team of volunteers or mentor a single volunteer? Ask a board member who has professional fundraising skills to help oversee your fundraising volunteers, guiding them to stretch their skills.

✓ Cooperate with a fellow nonprofit organization by sharing skilled mentors. Does another nonprofit have an extraordinary professional speaker? Is this person willing to mentor outreach volunteers within your nonprofit and help them polish their skills? Offer this nonprofit the same mentorship possibilities from your organization's leaders.

Guide Offers Menu of Mentor Training Options

Wondering where to start when it comes to training mentors? Follow this guide from Big Brothers Big Sisters of America (BBBSA) of Philadelphia, PA. This training module focuses on 10 areas of mentor training that you can apply to your own mentor program.

Developed in the early 1990s, the guide is really a menu of training options, says Joyce Corlett, director of program development. "It was designed as a cookbook for the agencies," Corlett says. "We were trying to make something the most sophisticated and least sophisticated at the same time."

Two hours of training can be devoted to each module. But, Corlett says most BBBS agencies pick areas to work on depending on their needs. For example, not every agency has time or resources to offer 20 hours of training for mentors. So some only pick a couple of the titles to use in training.

Corlett says the training module can actually be broken down into two parts: pre-match up and post-match up.

The four principles to focus on before mentors are matched with mentees are: relationship building, communication skills, values clarification and child development.

The additional titles work great for follow-up training, she says, because a mentor cannot predict every situation that will arise with their mentee, so these extra titles are available to keep supporting mentors in their role. These titles include: child abuse, substance abuse, sexuality, problem solving, and refocus and recharge.

"Mentoring youth can be daunting," says Corlett. "It's not as scary as people think, but it is important to put it into perspective."

Source: Joyce Corlett, Director of Program Development, Big Brothers Big Sisters of America, Philadelphia, PA. Phone (215) 665-7749. E-mail: jcorlett@bbbsa.org

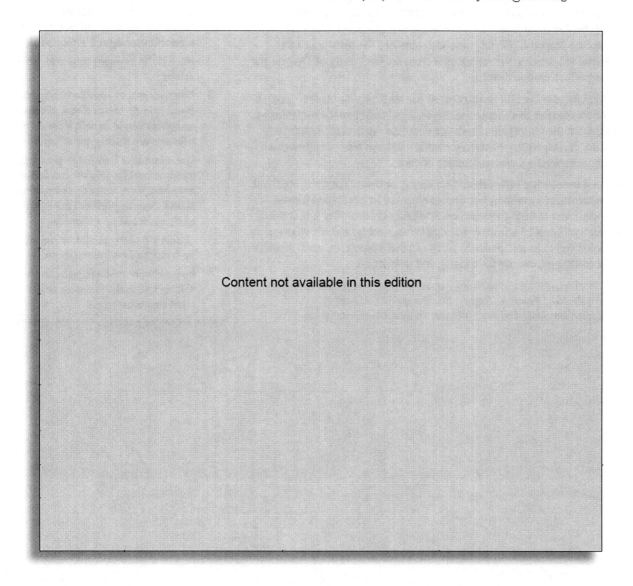

Content not available in this edition

E-mentor Program Broadens Organization's Reach

If mentors — volunteer or paid — play a significant role in your volunteer program, consider expanding your mentoring program with virtual options.

Offering e-mentoring allows staff and volunteers at Access to Student Assistance Programs in Reach of Everyone (ASPIRE) of Eugene, OR, to broaden their reach to constituents, says Lori Ellis, ASPIRE and outreach supervisor.

In the ASPIRE mentoring program, administered by the Oregon Student Assistance Commission, volunteer mentors help high school students get information and support regarding their college options. Begun in 1998 with four pilot sites, the program is branching out to reach 165 sites throughout Oregon by the end of the current school year.

Because of the challenges of signing on volunteers in more remote regions of the state, ASPIRE offers e-mentoring opportunities called eASPIRE that allow volunteers to reach students via the Web.

Ellis shares three issues to consider when looking to expand your mentoring services into the virtual world:

✓ **Virtual mentoring expands your program infinitely.** Since volunteers are not limited to a specific region, eASPIRE attracts volunteers from highly professional levels such as college professors. Through the remote mentoring program, officials have also obtained the assistance of a financial aid director, vice chancellor from the University of Oregon and a nonprofit executive director.

✓ **Virtual mentoring still requires real-life staff or volunteers.** Assign a site coordinator to evaluate the program and facilitate the e-mentoring program at the remote site. Train site coordinators or staff members to monitor correspondence between mentors and mentees to ensure that communications are appropriate and on task.

✓ **Virtual mentoring offers flexible training options.** Train site staff and volunteer mentors with live online webinars or in a recorded format they can view at their convenience. ASPIRE officials offer live webinar sessions offering 25 attendees training twice weekly, and are working on recorded webinars and podcasts (see box) that volunteers, staff, mentors and constituents can use for training and instruction.

Source: Lori Ellis, ASPIRE and Outreach Supervisor, Access to Student Assistance Programs in Reach of Everyone, Eugene, OR. Phone (800) 452-8807. E-mail: lorianne.m.ellis@state.or.us. Website: www.aspireoregon.org

Six Tips for Creating Podcasts

Creating video or audio podcasts on specific topics relevant to your mentors, volunteers and constituents is yet another way for your nonprofit to deliver strong service.

At Access to Student Assistance Programs in Reach of Everyone (ASPIRE), Eugene, OR, officials create podcasts to communicate effectively with constituents. ASPIRE is a mentoring program that offers volunteers the opportunity to mentor high school students regarding their college options.

Lori Ellis, ASPIRE and outreach supervisor, shares six tips for creating effective podcasts:

1. Create a template that includes a consistent opening and closing that supports your agency's mission.
2. Maintain an engaging tone and avoid a dry delivery.
3. Use podcasts to provide information about specific topics that a variety of audiences would benefit from or that will help provide training for volunteers.
4. Use short time frames for presenting information. Ellis says she has found that anywhere from three to seven minutes allows them to present information that is easily absorbed by audiences.
5. Create a podcast studio to record your podcasts to limit interruptions.
6. Invest in microphones, webcams and software to make the most of the recording experience.

Useful Policies, Examples and Forms for the Volunteer Manager

EFFECTIVELY UTILIZING VOLUNTEERS FOR SPECIAL EVENTS

Special events represent a unique volunteering opportunity. Community members are often more inclined to volunteer for a one-time event than an ongoing position, and nonprofits often need extra help producing their event. The following articles offer tips and hints on how to maximize this relationship and get the most out of your volunteer greeters, helpers, servers, organizers, and leaders.

Recruit and Manage Volunteers for Your Next Special Event

Recruiting special event volunteers allows your organization to plan events in an organized fashion with strong oversight. Officials with March of Dimes (Kalamazoo, MI) recruit special event volunteers to manage every detail of their events.

"The role of a special event volunteer is to serve the organization in a variety of capacities," says Dana DeLuca, March of Dimes division director. "Whether it be handling pre-event administrative tasks, serving as a committee member, cultivating event revenue or overseeing the event logistics, the special event volunteer is multi-faceted and plays an essential role in the overall success of an event. The most challenging task is finding the right role for each volunteer, managing to their strengths and giving them the tools to succeed and to feel successful."

DeLuca offers tips to recruit and manage special event volunteers:

❑ Make the ask. People can only respond if asked, and volunteer-minded persons are likely to offer something to your nonprofit. More often than not, says DeLuca, the volunteer with the most staying power has been asked to join the organization in a volunteer capacity to help move the mission forward.

❑ Determine the volunteer's specialty. Find what motivates each individual volunteer and assign him/her to opportunities according to those strengths. "It pays to find out what people are looking to gain from their role as volunteers and to help match them up with opportunities that best complement their desire to give back," says DeLuca.

❑ Give them the tools to succeed and get out of their way. Through the March of Dimes Volunteer Leadership Institute, an executive leadership program helps volunteers become experts in the organization. The program, DeLuca says, helps in recruiting and retaining strong board members, having successful events and providing effective programming. Tools offered to volunteers include educational items such as the publications shown at left that illustrate where gifts go and provide basic information about the March of Dimes so volunteers can speak in an informed way at special events.

Source: Dana DeLuca, Division Director, March of Dimes, Portage, MI. Phone (269) 343-5586. E-mail: ddeluca@marchofdimes.com. Website: www.marchofdimes.com/michigan

Content not available in this edition

Providing volunteers with educational items such as these helps prepare them to speak at special events on behalf of the March of Dimes (Portage, MI).

Special Event Flyer Combines Community Recruiting Efforts

Work with other area nonprofits to create a quarterly flyer that features special event volunteer opportunities. Title your flyer Special Event Volunteer Opportunities and distribute it to local media, public service websites, the chamber of commerce and other appropriate venues. Post it on each participating nonprofit's website and at local businesses.

To create the flyer, ask a representative of each participating nonprofit to complete one paragraph per event that includes:

❑ Brief description of the hosting organization and description of the event (including time, date and location).

❑ Available volunteer roles, as well as hours or list of shifts available.

❑ Age requirements or other volunteer specifications.

❑ Contact information, including name, title and phone number of appropriate person within your organization.

Share the task of compiling the list by rotating which agency will create and distribute the list each quarter.

Seven Tips to Recruit and Retain Special Event Volunteers

Produced by the La Quinta Arts Foundation (La Quinta, CA), the 29-year-old La Quinta Arts Festival is widely considered by both artists and art patrons alike to be one of the best annual festivals of its kind nationwide. The four-day event attracts about 20,000 visitors per year and has been named a Top 10 festival by numerous arts publications.

The arts festival is also one of the La Quinta Arts Foundation's biggest fundraisers.

Christi Salomone, the arts foundation's executive director, estimates about 300 volunteers work on the festival each year. Here, she shares seven ideas for recruiting and retaining a large number of dedicated volunteers for your large special events:

1. **Rely on word of mouth.** Although the foundation does recruit through various methods, Salomone says most festival volunteers come by way of experienced volunteers encouraging their friends, family and colleagues to join them.

2. **Use other community-based (and free) methods of recruitment.** "We post under 'Community' in the local newspaper, on our website and through social-media networks," Salomone says. "We give presentations at other service agencies (Rotary, etc.), and we take advantage of community newsletters."

3. **Always be recruiting.** "Many volunteers are introduced to our organization by attending and enjoying our events," Salomone says, "which leads them to want to play a role in an event's continuing success." Remember that every time the public turns out, that is an opportunity to recruit — and that every public event you produce should, therefore, show your best side.

4. **Look across the age spectrum.** "We are lucky to live in an area desirable to active retirees," says Salomone, which leads to a high turnout of older volunteers. Try focusing your volunteer-recruitment efforts at retirement centers, churches and the like. Another tactic: For volunteer duties that could be carried out by a family acting as a unit, pitch yourself to PTA groups, schools, or, again, churches. If you have teen-friendly volunteer duties, see if your local high school or church youth group can help you out, as some require young people to fulfill volunteer-service duties.

5. **Prepare them!** You'd be surprised how many nonprofits recruit volunteers for an event and then just tell them to show up. Not at La Quinta — volunteers are given written job descriptions and orientation meetings. Another amenity volunteers enjoy: assigned parking and/or parking passes.

6. **Assign everyone a leader.** A critical reason that the La Quinta Arts Festival's volunteers return year after year, according to Salomone is, "Our volunteers know that there is always a go-to staff person on whom they can rely to solve any issue."

7. **Thank volunteers the same as you do donors.** After all, time is money. "We acknowledge their contributions by imparting a personal touch," says Salomone, "such as a handwritten thank-you note. We find volunteers who feel their contributions are valued and have a good experience are likely to return year after year."

Source: Christi Salomone, Executive Director, La Quinta Arts Foundation, La Quinta, CA. Phone (760) 564-1244. E-mail: Christi@lqaf.com. Website: www.lqaf.com

EFFECTIVELY UTILIZING VOLUNTEERS FOR SPECIAL EVENTS

Low-tech Recruitment Method Brings in 500 Volunteers

Nearly 2,000 volunteers served at the Feed My Starving Children (Coon Rapids, MN) MobilePack™ food-packaging event, which took place Nov. 12-14, 2010.

Organized by 5th Bridge (Northfield, MN), a donor-focused organization whose mission is to enhance individual and community life in Northfield by encouraging the habits of volunteerism and philanthropy — the three-day volunteer event netted 534,600 meals for those in impoverished countries.

Organizers say a notably low-tech recruitment method helped draw a significant number of volunteers: placing clipboard sign-up sheets at local churches. Persons who signed up through this method numbered nearly 500, a full 25 percent of the total number of volunteers.

Candy Taylor, executive director of 5th Bridge, shares tips to maximize recruitment through clipboard placement:

- Place clipboards with sign-up sheets in the high-traffic areas of churches or other locations where your target volunteer audience is likely to frequent.

- At the top of each sheet include name of the volunteer event, clearly defined dates of service, shift parameters and any information about attire or details needed for volunteering.

- Ask enrollees to provide names, phone numbers and e-mail addresses when signing up for a volunteer shift.

- Leave slips of paper or note cards by the sign-up sheet so volunteers can note the day and time they signed on to serve.

- Leave literature about the cause near the clipboard sign-up forms to answer participant questions along with a note or placard encouraging volunteers to take the brochure or information with them.

- Appoint a representative at the church to take charge of gathering clipboards and sending e-mail reminders to participants at least two days prior to the event along with details about the shift the volunteer signed on to complete.

Source: Candy Taylor, Executive Director, 5th Bridge, Northfield, MN. Phone (507) 581-3017. E-mail: candy@5thbridge.org. Website: www.5thBridge.org

Formal Invitation Grabs Volunteer Prospects' Attention

Finding it difficult to get the attention of would-be volunteers? Send a formal invitation.

Formal invitations — particularly those that are hand-addressed — are generally the first items that get read as recipients review their daily mail.

Why not use a formal invitation, complete with RSVP, that requests the honor of their volunteer presence? Invite responders to attend an open house to meet your board, other volunteers and tour your facilities.

Your invitation's RSVP could even include a listing of project preferences for the individual to identify.

THE STAFF AND BOARD OF DIRECTORS
OF THE MONSON COUNTY HUMANE
SOCIETY
REQUEST YOUR PRESENCE
AT AN

OPEN HOUSE
THURSDAY, DECEMBER 1, 2011
5 TO 7 PM

TOUR THE FACILITIES
VISIT OUR LOVEABLE "CLIENTS"
AND
EXPLORE VOLUNTEER OPPORTUNITIES

✧ ✧ ✧

LOCATED AT 5TH & MCCLAY STREETS
HARRISON, ARIZONA

__ I (We) plan to attend the Open House at the Monson County Humane Society, Thursday, Dec. 1, 2011.

I (We) would like to learn more about the following volunteer opportunities:

❑ Animal care   ❑ Facility upkeep
❑ Membership   ❑ Transporation
❑ Special events   ❑ Ambassadors
❑ Clerical duties   ❑ Adoption
❑ Presentations   ❑ Publicity
❑ Other _____

❑ I (We) can't attend, but would like to learn more about volunteer opportunities at Monson County Humane Society.

❑ I (We) cannot attend or volunteer at this time.

Name(s): _____
_____

Use this sample to create your own agency-specific formal invitation.

Layer Subsequent Years' Events With New Responsibilities

The type of event doesn't really matter — fundraisers, workshops, reunions and more. Newly created events evolve one of two ways: 1) After a year or two, interest wanes and the event is dropped or; 2) the event builds year after year into a highly anticipated, well-attended occasion.

The direction an event takes is hugely dependent on the planners' level of enthusiasm for it and the degree to which volunteers become involved in owning it.

Assuming event planners are enthusiastic about its purpose and potential, be sure to add layers of volunteer involvement and ownership each year, being mindful not to divert attention from prior years' components. This will boost volunteer involvement, enthusiasm and attendance. With more volunteers, you can do more — offer child care, continuing education, tours, a reception, etc. — than was possible in previous years.

The minute you stop fine-tuning your volunteer events, enthusiasm will wane. Don't let that happen. Always be looking for volunteer-driven ways to improve events.

Seek Volunteer Input to Improve Your Annual Events

Asking volunteers to complete an evaluation form after a major event is an opportunity to improve your organization and engage your volunteers.

The Kansas State Historical Society (KSHS) of Topeka, KS, boasts a 300-member volunteer program. Volunteers assist KSHS in presenting Kansas Day activities that mark the state's annual birthday celebration. On average, nearly 2,000 people attend Kansas Day events with volunteers clocking in almost 400 hours of service, says Lois Herr, Kansas Day coordinator.

In 2011, as Kansas celebrates its 150th birthday, groups such as schools, civic organizations, youth groups, towns and counties will be part of a grassroots effort to commemorate the state's sesquicentennial. A KSHS Kansas Day toolkit designed to guide groups through the process of organizing public events includes the sample volunteer evaluation form (shown ar right).

The volunteer evaluation has three purposes, Herr says:

1. To find out how the individual's experience was;

2. To include the volunteer's input in evaluating the success of the event using the volunteer's eyes and ears; and

3. To collect recommendations on how the event can be improved.

She encourages other volunteer managers to create similar evaluation forms to engage their volunteers while improving events. "Introducing volunteer evaluation forms into your programs will offer you insights into the progress of your events through the eyes of your volunteers," Herr says. "You'll value their input, and they'll appreciate the opportunity to add value to your future events."

Source: Lois Herr, Kansas Day Coordinator, Kansas State Historical Society, Topeka, KS. Phone (785) 272-8681. E-mail: lherr@kshs.org. Website: www.kshs.org

This sample evaluation form, courtesy of Kansas State Historical Society (Topeka, KS), www.kshs.org, illustrates a simple way to engage volunteers while improving volunteer-driven events.

Content not available in this edition

Useful Policies, Examples and Forms for the Volunteer Manager

USEFUL VOLUNTEER POLICIES AND PROCEDURES

Volunteer programs are complex affairs, and no one resource could contain all the resources needed to ensure long-term success. Nevertheless, the policies and procedures appearing here — ranging from conflict of interest policies to volunteer sharing arrangements — cover several major issues and give an idea of the directions nonprofits can go in formulating their own policies.

Share Volunteers With Other Organizations

If you're having difficulty enlisting enough volunteers for your organization's demands, or if you're embarking on a special project that could use lots of extra hands, why not explore partnering with another organization that also utilizes volunteers?

You could establish an ongoing relationship in which volunteers could be shifted among participating agencies depending on the demands at hand. Or you could simply join forces for a one-time project that has positive results for each organization.

Here's how you can develop a possible collaboration with one or more agencies:

1. List all programs and projects you have (or would like to have) that involve volunteers. Separate ongoing programs from those covering a specified time period. This helps illustrate how many additional volunteers are needed and for what purposes.

2. Look at other organizations in your community or region that use volunteers. Which organizations — and their pools of volunteers — would make the best match with yours? Should you consider an organization totally different from yours (noncompetitive), or does it make sense to approach an organization with traits similar to yours?

3. As you narrow the list of possible organizations with which you could collaborate, weigh the possible benefits for each organization. Knowing which organizations could receive the greatest pay back will help determine the most likely candidates to approach.

4. Consider enlisting the assistance of a board member or volunteer leader in approaching the other organizations. If possible, encourage the organization officials to invite one of their board members or volunteers as well. Involving a board member or volunteer in exploring a collaborative effort helps overcome the politics of a possible partnership.

5. As you explore a volunteer partnership with another organization, identify benefits for both organizations as you walk through each cooperative project example. Also point out benefits for the participating volunteers as well. How might they benefit from a collaborative venture?

6. Anticipate potential obstacles that could arise from a collaborative effort and be prepared to offer solutions during your initial talks.

7. If the collaborative effort shows promise, develop a planning document outlining both mutual and individual responsibilities for each participating organization. If possible, assign responsibilities to appropriate individuals along with deadlines as well. Try to be as detailed as possible to avoid any confusion or misunderstanding on the part of participants.

Whatever your project or program, you can create a win-win partnership by joining volunteer forces, and both organizations will receive public praise for their ingenuity.

Make Volunteer Programs Outcome-oriented

Just as it's important to evaluate the effectiveness of all your organization's programs, it's equally important to measure those that are volunteer-driven to: 1) improve them, 2) affirm their effectiveness or 3) replace them.

Generally, each program should be evaluated annually and should measure outcomes on a quantitative and qualitative basis.

Here are some examples of outcomes you may wish to measure:

• **Individual and overall volunteer accomplishment toward stated objectives**: number of calls, amount raised, numbers served, contributed hours, etc.

• **Individual and overall volunteer satisfaction during the project**: attendance/absenteeism, results of volunteer satisfaction surveys, recognition, etc.

• **Effectiveness of volunteer recruitment**: comparative totals from year-to-year, number of new volunteers, volunteers per recruiter, recruitment structure, etc.

• **Effectiveness of volunteer retention**: comparative totals from year-to-year, changes in level of involvement/responsibility among volunteer veterans, etc.

• **Training effectiveness**: amount of time/materials committed to training, degree of staff involvement, level of volunteer understanding, etc.

Components of a Conflict of Interest Policy

Having a strong conflict of interest policy within your organization can protect your nonprofit — including its volunteers, from persons who answer the phones to persons who direct policy — from unnecessary scrutiny.

A conflict of interest occurs when an individual's obligation to further the organization's charitable purposes is at odds with his/her own financial interests. For example, a conflict of interest would occur when an officer, director or trustee votes on a contract between the nonprofit and a business owned by that officer according to the Internal Revenue Service (IRS) website at www.irs.gov/charities.

Having officers, boards of directors, volunteer managers and volunteers sign a conflict of interest form can be the best method of prevention. The IRS site goes on to clarify, "Apart from any appearance of impropriety, organizations will lose their tax-exempt status unless they operate in a manner consistent with their charitable purposes."

To create a strong conflict of interest policy, add the following components to your document to clarify your organization's demand for professionalism among your constituents and officers:

❑ Specify whom the policy is meant to direct.

❑ Include a section stating areas where conflicts have been known to or can easily arise.

❑ Include a section that depicts examples or possible conflict of interest scenarios.

❑ Specify disclosure procedure when a conflict of interest is identified.

❑ Include a signatory area that clearly defines that the member or officer read and understands the policy and the capacity in which that person acts within the organization. Allow space for a member or officer to divulge any current or perceived conflict of interest.

❑ Consider posting your conflict of interest policy on your website.

Find a sample conflict of interest policy at the Minnesota Attorney General's Office website at www.ag.state.mn.us/Charities/ to use as a guide when creating your policy.

Promote Wellness Among Your Co-workers, Volunteers

June marks Professional Wellness Month, when professionals are encouraged to reflect on the work they do and how they may find balance and become more effective in their positions.

Carry this idea forward to your staff, volunteers and others to bring awareness to the necessary work they do and promote activities that positively impact their health and well-being.

One simple way to promote wellness among your volunteers and the persons they work with is to stock the breakroom or workroom with healthful snack choices such as fresh fruit and vegetables. June also happens to be National Fruit and Vegetables Month allowing for a natural tie-in for health and wellness promotion.

Here are a few more ideas for promoting wellness at your nonprofit:

❑ Encourage a fit lifestyle for staff and volunteers by creating opportunities to focus on physical wellness. Consider asking a weight-loss organization such as Weight Watchers to offer on-site meetings. Offer

opportunities for colleagues to gather for physical fitness by organizing a walking or cardio-fitness group.

❑ Promote stress reduction internally. Staff and volunteers who are on the low end of the stress spectrum will better serve constituents and members. Try promoting stress reduction by giving out stress balls or by promoting stress therapy through massage, yoga or general stretching techniques.

❑ Encourage worksite organization by providing staff and volunteers with desk organizers, planners, recycling bins or other items that will promote tidiness and efficiency. Organized individuals will surely be less stressed.

❑ Promote a positive environment by offering staff and volunteers the opportunity to share ways to better serve clients or members in a more efficient manner. Create an outlet for responses whether that's devoting an internal blog to idea sharing or setting up a suggestion box. Emphasize that only positive ideas will be considered and create a system of recognizing workable ideas by offering small prizes.

Partner With Other Nonprofits to Share Volunteer Strength

Ever explore various ways your volunteers might collaborate with volunteers from one or more other agencies to tackle a big project? Consider the following collaborative scenarios for projects that require large numbers of volunteers to help:

- Agree to a project exchange — Your volunteers agree to assist another agency with a onetime project in exchange for their volunteers helping you with a onetime effort.

- Create a volunteer hours exchange with another organization — If there are various times you need extra assistance throughout the year, partner with another organization to exchange volunteer assistance based on contributed time, say 500 hours per year. You can utilize as many volunteers as you need as often as you need them.

- Organize a fundraiser with another nonprofit — relying on volunteers from both — and split the proceeds. (This is a great way to expose new people to your cause.)

Prepare Staff Before Placing Volunteers

Once staff members request volunteer assistance and you supply needed personnel, do staff know what to do at that point? When volunteers show up, will the staff member in charge support them in a way consistent with your expectations?

If you are going to supply departments with needed volunteers, it's important they accommodate those unpaid helpers in a professional manner. Here's how to help:

1. Insist that any personnel desiring volunteer assistance first participate in a brief workshop designed to show the dos and dont's of working with volunteers.

2. When requests are made for volunteer assistance — and such requests should be encouraged — have a process in place that allows you to get all of the needed facts before enlisting help: How many volunteers will be required? What will they be expected to do? Who will be on hand to assist them or answer questions? What is the time frame of the assigned task(s)? Are there any special qualifications?

3. If possible, check up on the volunteers to be sure everything is going as expected. In addition, be sure they know they can come to you if they have a problem or question that is not being addressed by the department for which they are working.

4. Have a system in place that allows you to survey both volunteers and staff as part of your evaluation of the completed project. Knowing perceptions of both staff and volunteers enables you to make needed improvements.

Help Fellow Employees Appreciate the Value of Volunteers

Helping colleagues understand the key role volunteers can and do play will strengthen existing volunteer-driven programs and make new initiatives possible.

If your employees begin to recognize the contributions being made by existing volunteers, they may identify new opportunities for volunteer involvement in their own areas of responsibility. In addition, the more all employees recognize the contributions being made by existing volunteers, the more they will join in directing appreciation to them and, as a result, help to retain them.

Decide which of these practical strategies you can implement to help your employees better recognize volunteer contributions:

- Regularly list accomplishments/services of volunteers in your in-house newsletter.

- Make use of a volunteer bulletin board that showcases volunteers and their work.

- Invite a volunteer to speak during an employee meeting, describing his/her duties.

- Create a video — depicting your volunteers in action — that can be checked out by employees and used as a recruitment tool as well.

- Conduct an in-house survey that identifies new volunteer opportunities.

Lightning Source UK Ltd.
Milton Keynes UK
UKOW01f0822020813

214783UK00006B/159/P